English Manor Houses

*Haddon Hall, Derbyshire. The Great Hall, showing screens passage, minstrels'
gallery and doors to service rooms*

English Manor Houses

by

BRIAN BAILEY

ROBERT HALE · LONDON

To
my Mother and Father,
and
my Mother-in-Law

© *Brian Bailey 1983*
First published in Great Britain 1983

ISBN 0 7090 1280 2

Robert Hale Limited
Clerkenwell House
Clerkenwell Green
London, EC1

Photoset by Rowland Phototypesetting Ltd
Printed in Great Britain by
St Edmundsbury Press, Bury St Edmunds, Suffolk
Bound by Woolnough Bookbinding Ltd

Contents

Illustrations

Acknowledgements

Acknowledgement is made to the following for their kind permission to reproduce copyright photographs on the pages stated. *A. F. Kersting*: frontispiece, 16, 18, 26, 27, 35, 41, 43, 45, 46, 48, 51, 52, 58, 64, 66, 73, 74, 77, 78, 82, 88, 90, 92, 97, 101, 104, 106, 108, 115, 117, 122, 134, 135, 141, 142, 144, 146, 153, 154, 156, 158, 166, 168, 171, 180, 181, 185 (below), 187, 188, 193, 197, 201, 203, 204, 208, 212, 213, 215, 230, 232, 235, 238, 239. *Cambridge University Collection*: 19. *Brian Davison*: 28. *Kenneth Scowen*: 38, 130, 195. *Leicestershire Museums*: 50. *Rita Bailey*: 96. *Salford Museums & Art Galleries*: 114. *Bournville Village Trust*: 118. *Metropolitan Borough of Stockport*: 176. *Kirklees Metropolitan Council*: 185 (above). The remaining photographs are the author's.

Acknowledgements

Apart from the writers whose previous researches have been of immense help, and who are listed at the end of the book, my greatest debt is to those owners of manor houses whose properties I have been able to see, but I should add at once that I have not seen all the houses mentioned in the book, and I have seen a great many more from the outside than I have seen from the inside.

My wife has contributed a great deal by driving me everywhere and enabling me to see a large number of manor houses in a relatively short time. Without her willing co-operation I would have taken much longer to complete the book.

I am grateful to Mr Van Phillips for twenty-six volumes of Pevsner without which I should have had to do a lot more of my research in the relatively less comfortable surroundings of reference libraries.

Introduction

In many hundreds of villages throughout England, the oldest and most important surviving building after the church is the manor house. It may not be called that. The local people may refer to it as 'the old hall' or 'the big house'. Sometimes it has been relegated to use as a farmhouse, or a vicarage, or an hotel, or it may be in ruins, but it nearly always holds a special place in the affections of the older people who, even if they know very little of its history and regard those who occupy it now as complete strangers, have a sense of its past influence on the growth of their village. The collective unconscious preserves the memory of an institution which has become an anachronism, and the building stands – perhaps in splendid isolation; perhaps beside the church or the village green – as a relic of a past which everyone is curious about but no one wants back.

The English manor house may be seen as a symbol of several things – of relatively peaceful times after the stormy centuries between the departure of the Romans and the arrival of the Normans; of the growth of a class system and a conservative tradition; of an organized and disciplined approach to labour. What it cannot symbolize is democracy. As democratic institutions grew, manor houses faded out.

Compared with castles and stately homes, and even with vernacular architecture, manor houses have not received their due in literature, yet they often possess a charm of their own which is quite missing from other domestic buildings, whether larger or smaller. The spacious ostentation which makes the vast homes of princes and dukes awe-inspiring to the average mortal who spends his own life in rustic simplicity or semi-detached urbanism, does not often overwhelm one in the homes of lords of the manors. They are generally more intimate and cosy than the huge mansions of the higher nobility, and it is easier to identify with their inhabitants through the centuries of occupation. Even when a manor house is very old and neglected and has about it that musty odour which seems to distinguish it as the ancestral home of the death-watch beetle rather than of a noble family, one easily grasps the daily life which, in a palace or a castle, seems remote from reality.

The history of many genuine and so-called manor houses is obscure, however, and we must proceed with caution. Many a house with the name 'Manor' is not, and many a so-called 'Castle' *is* a genuine manor house. There is no infallible guide, but a house with the name 'Hall' or 'Old Hall' is quite likely to be a real manor house, whilst one with the name 'Place' or 'Court' is probably not. To confuse matters still further, some stately homes, which are certainly not manor houses now (even in the historical or architectural sense, which are the only senses in which *any* building is a manor house today) were so once and may have the original manor houses incorporated in their structures.

The interpretation of 'manor house' for this book is a fairly catholic one, anyway. In the early chapters, it is possible to define the term strictly. A building which was lived in permanently or intermittently by a feudal baron, provided it was not a castle, was a manor house. But as feudalism died, the meaning of the term 'manor house' became fogged, and as time went on, it became hallowed by tradition but of increasingly doubtful accuracy. Although the occupants of these houses in later times liked to think of themselves as lords of manors, and were regarded as such by their subservient tenants and neighbours, their estates were not manors, and they were usually not lords. But the courtesy title persisted, and as a general rule, I have taken 'manor house' to mean the home of a country landowner exercising the remnants of manorial rights over his tenants or villagers, as distinct from a man of property who merely owns a house in the country.

Any discussion of English manor houses must, in any case, be very selective, and my aim is to weave a roughly chronological course through these hubs of the social history of rural England from the Dark Ages to the Industrial Revolution. It should be noted that relatively few of the houses mentioned in the book are open to the public. In particular, very few of the most ancient survivals, which in some ways are the most interesting, can normally be seen. But more owners of historic buildings are opening their homes each year. Some of those manor houses which are open regularly can be found in the Appendix.

A final word concerns the spelling of family names. The inconsistency which sometimes occurs is absolved by tradition, and I have not changed the spelling of a name on a fifteenth-century tombstone in order to make it conform to the spelling used by the same family three hundred years later.

CHAPTER 1

The Origins of the Manor House

Those who like neat and tidy answers to difficult questions suppose that the manor originated with the new beginning which the Anglo-Saxons brought to the story of Britain. And as an institution, it undoubtedly did, although it is worth pointing out that the word 'manor' is of French origin and was only introduced into the English language after the Norman Conquest. The real origins of the manor house are, in any case, more tricky than that.

Although some historians have long implied that the Anglo-Saxons wiped the British slate clean and made a completely fresh start to life on this island, common sense tells us that this is a half-truth. People's habits and beliefs are not easily changed, even in the course of centuries, and nothing short of genocide could achieve such a clean sweep. Anglo-Saxons may have imposed a new economic system on this country, but they must also have absorbed a great deal of what they found here already. It seems probable that the whole idea of private property, and therefore of different classes of society, was taken over from Roman civilization, since the barbarian tribes of northern Europe, whence the Angles and Saxons came, probably held and administered their land on a communal basis.

The manor's foundations, as it were, may well have been laid during the Roman occupation. The evidence is much debated, but we ought to note the possibility that the Roman villa was the predecessor, in spirit at any rate, of the English manor house. In the lowland arable areas of Britain – southern England, East Anglia and the south Midlands – some Romano-British villas certainly seem to have been the administrative centres of large agricultural estates. Their owners may have been retired Roman officers in some cases, and wealthy Britons in others, but it seems likely, in any event, that much of the land was worked by natives who were little better than slaves, whilst other land was let to tenants who, by the fourth century, as Sheppard Frere has written, 'had become bound to the soil like medieval serfs under

Athelhampton, Dorset. Characteristic ornaments of the medieval great hall – tapestry, weapons and hunting trophies

a hereditary tie, paying rent in kind as often as in money, and occasionally, at any rate, having customary obligations of part-time work on what may loosely be described as manorial lands'.

Tacitus remarked in his *Germanica* on the personal loyalty which local chiefs in the Germanic lands could command from their followers, and it seems fairly obvious that what began as an almost instinctive need of leadership among barbarian tribes in battle was gradually moulded into an equally unquestioning way of life in rural economy. So far from imposing an entirely new system on their subject-peoples, the Anglo-Saxons may only have exploited the growing habits of the British, some of

Chedworth, Gloucestershire. A centrally heated Roman villa which was the headquarters of a large agricultural estate

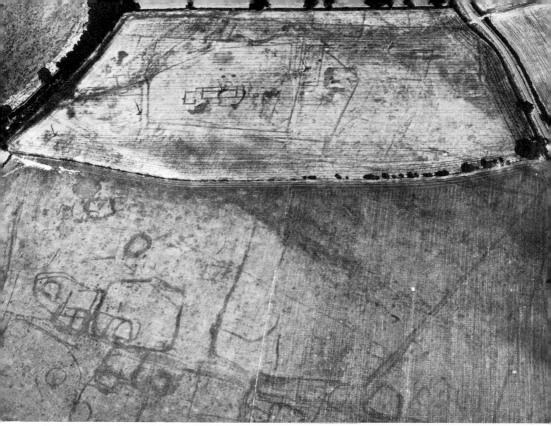

Lockington, Leicestershire. Aerial photography reveals enclosures and hut-circles which may have been occupied by peasant workers on the estate of the nearby Roman villa

which had been picked up during the centuries of Roman rule.

The Romans introduced what they called '*patrocinium*', for instance, in which a poor freeman was able to claim shelter and protection from a wealthy landowner in return for his services on the land. No military service was involved in this relationship, but the cradle of historical feudalism is evident in the institution. What is more, some villas seem to have been occupied not by the landlord himself but by his bailiff – another precedent for a common medieval practice.

Even the actual buildings of later manors had their predecessors – in idea if not in execution – in Romano-British villas. Among the more primitive type was the so-called basilican villa which was a large hall divided by timber posts into a nave and aisles, like a church, in which family and livestock both lived. This was the basis of the aisled hall of medieval England; whilst the layout of a more advanced villa such as that at Ditchley,

Oxfordshire, where a ditch enclosed a sort of courtyard with a dwelling house, well and barn, is not dissimilar to a manor house built over a thousand years later, such as Stokesay Castle, Shropshire, where a moat enclosed a courtyard with a dwelling house, well and kitchen block.

We cannot say with certainty, therefore, that the manor house was entirely a product of the medieval feudal system, and in any case, the Germanic invaders who became known as the English had themselves been exposed to Roman influence before they came here. But the historical manor house – the nucleus of the medieval lord's manor or demesne – is first encountered in the Anglo-Saxon period.

Tradition has it that a British chieftain named Vortigern sought the aid of the Saxons in repelling Picts and Scots who raided the country deserted by Rome, but the Saxons became ambitious and began that long process of piracy and plunder, turning their weapons upon their confederates, as Bede put it, which ended in the establishment of the English kingdom.

The English divided the land into administrative areas, each of which was called a '*scir*' – division. The *scirs* or shires were divided into 'hundreds' (or wapentakes, as they were called under the Danelaw) for judicial and taxation purposes. The hundreds in turn comprised many villages, or vills, but these were only accommodation areas – the important components of the hundreds, in most parts of England, were the manors.

Sometimes the manor and the village were the same thing, but more often than not, they differed widely, especially in the Danelaw, where the village was independent of the manor. Elsewhere, one manor might include several villages, whilst another might be divided between two or more manors. The sizes of manors varied from tiny demesnes to huge areas, the largest having two or three plough-teams per square mile, while the smallest might have only one ox to its name. It follows that the manor houses similarly varied enormously according to the wealth of the lord and the size of his holdings.

Before we look at manor houses in detail, therefore, it would be as well to have in our minds some idea of the social organization upon which the buildings depended. The old words for the different classes of people in Anglo-Saxon society have been used almost interchangeably and can be very confusing. The subtleties of distinction are still not understood precisely, but the following table gives a simplified picture of the social order:

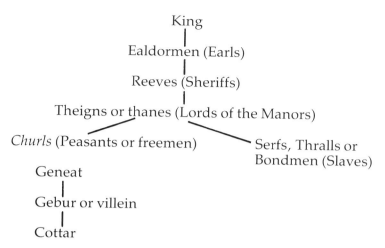

King
|
Ealdormen (Earls)
|
Reeves (Sheriffs)
|
Theigns or thanes (Lords of the Manors)

Churls (Peasants or freemen)   Serfs, Thralls or Bondmen (Slaves)

Geneat
|
Gebur or villein
|
Cottar

The economic basis of the feudal system was slavery. The lowest classes of early medieval society may be variously referred to as peasants, serfs or villeins, but whatever name we give them, they were all in reality little more than slaves, subject to ruthless exploitation by the lords. Many of them were, in theory, free men, but few owned any property, and most had no right of existence except as beasts of labour who were fed and sheltered by their owners in order to keep them fit for work. They were subject to the lord's private justice. The lord's jurisdiction (in theory) stopped short of capital offences, except that if a thief was caught red-handed, his lord was entitled to hang him. Men might, however, be punished by flogging or mutilation, and although there was some control over selling slaves to foreigners, male and female peasants were in practice sold to the Danes or sent abroad, although, oddly enough, peasants in the Danelaw had more freedom than those in the Anglo-Saxon territories. Freemen were in the majority in the Viking regions, where open field cultivation was less common. If the manor was transferred to another owner, the serfs went with it, as chattels. A serf had a fixed monetary value, and if he was murdered, or stolen, it was sufficient that his original owner should be paid that amount in compensation. That was all the law required.

Relief from slavery was very slow in coming, and even the abortive Peasants' Revolt was a long way off. Towards the end of the ninth century, Alfred the Great made a law which permitted slaves to own a little property and gave them a small number of 'holidays', on which they were entitled to sell property or earn money in their 'spare time'. The Church, meanwhile, enjoined everyone to treat serfs with humanity and held up as an act of Christian piety the freeing of any slave. But the Church's own wealth depended on the system, so it could hardly be counted on to condemn the principle, and St Thomas Aquinas passed off slavery as being the result of sin – a rationalization echoed in Chaucer's *Canterbury Tales* where the parson says that 'the condicioun of thraldom and the firste cause of thraldom is for sinne.'

Above the serf in the social scale was the so-called freeman, or churl. In theory (once again) he owned sufficient land in the open fields to provide for his family by his own means, though he was not bound to the soil as the serf was but might be a craftsman such as a blacksmith or carpenter. He could leave his property to his descendants, but if his land was barren, he might have to lease more land from his lord and pay for it either with his labour or with his produce. In any case, he owned a military duty to his lord, and some evidence of personal loyalty, not only of the peasant to his lord but of the lord to his men, seems to me to have led to much romanticizing of the relationship between lord and peasant.

The highest class of freeman was the geneat, or 'companion', who served the lord in the office of bailiff or bodyguard and paid rent for the property he occupied. Lower down the ladder the gebur, or villein, had his land as a gift from the lord and, in return for being set up with such as a pair of oxen, six sheep and necessary tools and utensils, had to work at least two days a week on the lord's land, plough an acre a week in the autumn and pay rent in money and in kind. On his death, all his property reverted to the lord of the manor.

Lowest of the so-called freemen was the cottar, or cottage-dweller, who held only the minimum amount of land and paid for it in service to the lord. In terms of living standards, the distinction between a cottar and a serf is probably academic. Even among the better-off churls, only a few would have owned a full team of eight oxen with which to plough their strips of land, and co-operation with their neighbours was born of necessity.

Those who presided over this miserable state of affairs were the noblemen, or thanes, and it is with them that we are chiefly concerned in the present context. They were essentially soldiers rather than farmers and generally became landowners by gift from the King for services rendered. Their obligations to the

King were military service, construction of fortifications and the maintenance of roads and bridges, as well as such occasional duties as providing a bodyguard, equipping a ship or making fences round a royal hunting ground.

A thane might be the lord of one manor or of many, and if he owned several manors, they might be widely dispersed. He could not live on them all at the same time, so the manor house on many an estate was occupied by the lord's agent or bailiff. Women of the nobility could also own estates by inheritance or widowhood.

The peasants could inherit nothing without paying a fine – called a 'heriot' – to the lord. They must also pay a fine if they sold an ox or a sheep. No maiden could be married without the consent of the lord, but if he gave it, a fine was due for this, too. Peasant orphans who were wards of the barons saw the profits from their fathers' lands going into the lords' pockets until they were considered old enough to run the properties for themselves – boys at twenty-one, girls at fourteen (for they were then of marriageable age).

It was possible for a superior churl (the Anglo-Saxon word puts the lower classes as onomatopoeically in their places as the Roman 'plebeian') to aspire to the ranks of the nobility. If he worked hard and prospered and owned at least five hides of land, he might have his 'wergild' – his monetary worth – raised to that of a thane, so that it was an expensive luxury for an enemy to kill him. And he might be made a thane, which was in the gift of the king's ealdormen. Land was the primary factor in the Anglo-Saxon economy, however. It did not matter how wealthy a peasant was through his resourcefulness or by his craftsmanship – if he did not own the requisite five hides of land, he could not enter the nobility. Nor was his title hereditary at first. Only after three generations had held the land were the family offspring born to the rank of thane.

Not all manors were the property of thanes, of course. Earls, bishops and abbots were also lords of manors, to say nothing of the King himself. Christian England was not far advanced in years before the Church was the biggest landowner next to the monarch. And manors were by no means evenly distributed throughout England, as we shall see.

The manor house was the administrative headquarters of an agricultural estate which might be quite modest or very extensive. The lord's own land, or 'demesne', might be in one parcel adjacent to the manor house, or it might be distributed among the strips in the open fields. As enclosure took place in later centuries, barons had their own farms near their manor houses, and these are often called 'Home Farm' or 'Manor Farm' to this day. (The farm in Orwell's satirical masterpiece is called Manor Farm after the one in the Hertfordshire village where he lived at the time.)

Most of the people who worked on the lord's land lived in villages, which grew up within easy reach of a water supply and which were surrounded by or adjacent to the two or three large open or common fields. The fields were divided and cultivated on a rotational system. Up to a point, the number of strips a man had depended on how many oxen he could afford to contribute to the plough teams, but he had to work on the lord's land as well as his own, and hard work on heavy clay soil with primitive tools seems to have led to a high proportion of leg and wrist fractures. If he was a villager, the peasant lived in hardly more than a hovel, if he was very poor, or perhaps in a hut of rectangular shape with walls of wattle and daub and a thatched roof supported on timber posts.

In theory, and to some extent, the peasant farmers were a self-governing community. They decided among themselves what crops should be grown, which field was to be left fallow and how to co-operate in getting all the strips ploughed with the oxen they could muster between them. But in practice, they were virtually owned by the lord of the manor, and as time went on, the situation became worse for them, not better. The Normans tried to simplify the confusing classes of society they found during the Domesday survey, recognizing only aristocracy and common people, or lords and vassals, but the general result was that there were fewer freemen in Norman times than there had been in the Anglo-Saxon period, and it would be splitting hairs to argue that the power of the lord over the lives of the people was anything other than despotism.

There is plenty of evidence that there was a strong bond of loyalty in Anglo-Saxon *ideals* between a lord and his men in times of war, and that it was regarded almost as a mortal sin for a soldier to survive a battle in which his lord had been killed. One cannot help wondering if there was a primeval thread linking the practice of *suttee* among Indian Brahmin widows with the Germanic obligation for a man whose lord had been slain to expose himself to death rather than be regarded as disloyal. Typical expressions of an almost ritual self-sacrifice are found in Anglo-Saxon literature: 'I will not run away, but shall lie dead alongside my lord. . . .' 'The brave warriors . . . will have no need to reproach me, now that my friendly lord lies dead, that I went home lordless or left the scene of the battle; but weapons shall end my life, spear-point and sword-blade.'

It goes without saying that it was not incumbent on a lord to invite death if one of his men was killed, though it was held proper for him to avenge the death, or at any rate to exact the man's wergild from his executioner!

As always, of course, romance was somewhat removed from reality. We have one telling story of a Northumbrian lord who was so tyrannical that he had great difficulty in keeping men to cultivate his land. One man, driven to desperation, is alleged to have enlisted the aid of St Cuthbert, Bishop of Lindisfarne, in escaping the manorial servants after he had loaded his cart with his belongings and fled with his family by night, taking his oxen and sheep with him. Generally speaking, however, the lord used his peasants and his slaves to line his own pockets – not only their labour and their produce but their very bodies.

The lord's house in Anglo-Saxon times, where his family and his retainers lived, was generally built of timber. In the earliest days, it consisted of a single-storey building – a great hall – with detached 'bowers' where the lord's family slept and performed their domestic offices, all enclosed within a defensive earthwork and perhaps a stockade, which made the property a kind of primitive fortified residence.

We ought to take notice at this point of a different opinion about the Saxon lord's domestic arrangements, which holds that the lord and his family did not use the hall all the time but only for public purposes. This view is based partly on the fact that there seems to have been no direct access as a rule from the hall to the solar, so that the lord and his wife and children would have got wet every time they passed from one to the other in the rain. Surely, it is argued, they would normally have lived in the solar and had their meals served there, and only brought the hall and its hearth into use when the occasion demanded.

What is certain, in any case, is that Saxon thanes lived in considerably less civilized conditions than their Roman counterparts had done, and that interest in building houses declined dramatically in Britain during the early Dark Ages. It is probable that in many cases these houses had no walls. They would be of the type called '*Grubenhäuser*' in Germany, in which the floor was below ground level in a shallow pit. The roof timbers would come right down to ground level and form a kind of tent, with a

Tapestries in the Punch Room of Cotehele House, Cornwall

doorway at one end. The huge roof, steeply pitched and thatched, would run off rain and snow quickly, and from this practice grew the knowledge and craftsmanship that enabled later medieval carpenters to build the awesome roofs of timber which survive in halls, barns and churches today.

The huge timber posts which supported the roofs of the halls also created aisles on either side, and in these the domestic animals might be kept at night, as well as the lord's slaves, minstrels, cooks, falconer and the like. Oxen, goats and dogs shared the hall with men, women and children, who ate their meals at benches whilst the lord and his family dined at one end of the hall and threw scraps to the dogs in a noisy and malodorous feast not helped by smoke from the fire on the central hearth escaping only half-heartedly through a louvre in the roof. The aisles seem to have had benches fixed round the walls as a rule, and they would be used as beds by the servants when the lord and his family had retired.

The epic poem *Beowulf*, probably written in the eighth century, provides a graphic description of the activity in the hall:

Penshurst Place, Kent. The medieval hall showing the central hearth

When evening came
Hrothgar departed to his private bower,
the king to his couch; countless were the men
who watched over the hall, as they had often done before.
They cleared away the benches, and covered the floor
with beds and bolsters. . . .

On the benches aloft . . .
were the ring-stitched mail-coat, the mighty helmet
steepling above the fray, and the stout spear-shaft.
It was their habit always, at home or on campaign,
to be ready for war, in whichever case,
whatsoever the hour might be
that the need came on their lord.

Beowulf describes a royal great hall with polished floors and
open hearth, walls of timber and lofty gables, ostensibly in

*Sulgrave, Northamptonshire. A stone wall of the Saxon thane's hall excavated in
1968. Its preservation is due to its being buried in the ramparts of a Norman earthwork
castle*

Denmark but probably of the same style as was being built on a smaller scale in the Viking territories of northern England. It also mentioned tapestries on the walls, and there is evidence enough that this was a common form of interior decoration in English noblemen's houses.

The probable hall of a thane, excavated at Sulgrave in Northamptonshire under the direction of Mr Brian Davison and dating from the eleventh century, was apparently centred on a great hall built of timber, without aisles but with a central hearth and a screened-off service area. At right angles to it was a chamber block with stone footings, and this may have had an upper storey. The building is a significant find, for two reasons, in particular. It is often thought that the Anglo-Saxons used stone for building only their later churches. Anglo-Saxon writers occasionally refer to the ruins of the Roman occupation as 'giants' work', meaning that they themselves were incapable of such building feats. A description of an eleventh-century carpenter at work on a house tells us how he first surveys the site, then cuts the timber 'and fits fairly the sills, and lays the beams and fastens the rafters to the ridge-pole, and supports it with buttresses, and afterwards he pleasantly decorates the house'. But it becomes clear from Sulgrave and other clues, not only that the profession of stone-mason was encroaching on that of carpenter from about the time of Alfred the Great, for other buildings as well as churches, but that both stone and timber buildings were sometimes given upper storeys. Inexperience, or shoddy workmanship, was not unknown, however. The Anglo-Saxon Chronicle records that in 978, 'the leading councillors of England fell down from an upper storey at Calne, all except the holy archbishop Dunstan, who alone remained standing on a beam: some were severely injured there, and some did not escape with their lives.'

Many other buildings may have just fallen down, for all we know, but the fact that a good many from seven or eight hundred years ago are still standing is remarkable enough when we consider that the masons and carpenters who put them up did so without benefit of architects, surveyors, slide-rules, laboratory information on stresses, or academic theories of aesthetics.

There are indications that some noblemen's houses of the Anglo-Saxon period were boat-shaped. That is, their long halls were wider in the middle than at the ends. The reasons for this are far from clear, but it may have had something to do with the buttressing and stability of timber buildings in gale-force winds.

The Bayeux Tapestry shows that two-storey buildings were not uncommon by the time of the Norman Conquest, especially in the towns, and because a first-floor hall gave its occupants a little security in times of political unrest, it soon became a more popular type of manor house than the aisled ground-floor hall, judging from the surviving examples.

Another obvious form of security was the moat, but this device served other practical purposes as well as defence. It could be used as a source of water for extinguishing fires in the timber and thatched buildings and for watering livestock; and it could be stocked with fish for the lord's table. It also provided drainage – a moated manor house with a built-in privy usually sited it so that it drained into the moat, and it is difficult to believe that the moat ever served that function to the exclusion of the others.

The Domesday survey of William the Conqueror provides information about the distribution of manors and their values in a time from which no manor houses survive. It was a kind of means test, carried out in such minute detail by William's French clerks that it was much resented by the native English, and it was they who nicknamed the resulting documents 'Domesday Book', for a survey of the country which left out of account not 'one hide or yard of land, nor even . . . an ox, or a cow, or a swine . . .' seemed to them very much like the Day of Judgement.

The total annual land value of England, except for the four northern shires which were not covered by the survey, was estimated at £73,000. Of this, more than half was owned by the King and the Church. In fact, *all* land was Crown property, and that held by others was 'enfeoffed' to them by the King in return for services rendered and expected. The 'others' in 1086 consisted of a very small number of favoured English landowners and about 170 French barons rewarded with land for their part in the conquest.

The most powerful landowners were those whose loyalty William knew (or thought) he could count on. His half-brother Robert, Count of Mortain, had eight hundred manors, chiefly in the south-west. Henry de Ferrers, one of the Domesday commissioners, had 114 manors in Derbyshire and nearly a hundred others scattered about in various parts of the country. Against such vast holdings as these, however, must be recorded the fact that, not only did some lords have only one manor, but some manors were tiny in the extreme. One in Devonshire possessed only one man and one ox.

It was a shrewd move of William's to distribute each baron's holdings of land widely. It meant that their interests coincided with those of other barons in different parts of England and made for a stable system. Land was the chief currency of the kingdom, and the landlords in their turns made smaller grants of land to the knights and others whom it was their duty to maintain in readiness for war when it occurred.

Since land was wealth, no landowner was willing to neglect any part of his holdings and risk its passing into other hands, however inconveniently distant it might be from his headquarters, and among the duties of the knights, when they were not in the king's service, was that of travelling with their lords about their scattered manors. The wealthier a lord was, the more time he had to spend in travelling. A great household on the move must have been quite a spectacle in those days. Accompanying the lord and his family would be his private army as well as his personal attendants – his steward, falconer, master of the horse and assorted servants, who might have to carry with them items of furniture, such as beds, as well as clothing, and tapestries to hang on the walls of the manor house which was their destination, for a lord with several manors would not leave valuable tapestries in all his unoccupied houses. The huge cost and upheaval of moving from manor to manor throughout the year must have influenced the gradual trend towards renting land to tenant farmers rather than direct management by the lord himself, or his bailiff. But that tendency was a long way off yet.

William's most trustworthy barons were given military commands in the most vulnerable parts of the country – the southeast coast, the Welsh Marches, the northern border – where they built their castles, in timber at first on the motte-and-bailey plan, and later in stone, with moats and drawbridges. The majority of manorial lords, however, were neither wealthy nor powerful enough to command castles, and they had to make do with manor houses which were sometimes very small indeed. Not that the castle owners had much greater comfort, nor much greater sophistication. The common language of the Norman aristocracy was French in speech and Latin in writing. Indeed, French was still spoken among the aristocracy in England until the fourteenth century, although by then it had become their second language. At least until the reign of Henry II, however, the average baron was as illiterate as the native villein.

The daily life of the lord of the manor in the eleventh century was much as one might expect of a soldier who comes into unaccustomed wealth and has no wars to fight. There was much promiscuity and drunkenness, and little privacy, and relief from the tedium came in the form of hunting and jousting. It was not until 1194 that jousting tournaments were controlled and licensed – before then they were informally organized mock-battles, though the blood spilled was real enough.

The lords derived their income from two chief sources, which may be generalized as their agricultural produce, on the one hand, and the rents of their tenants, on the other. But the variety of manorial work was great, and a lord in the south-east growing wheat and barley, and perhaps making ale or cider, was not necessarily better off than one in the Midlands breeding sheep and cattle and selling wool and dairy produce.

The lord's duties included presiding over regular manorial courts in which minor offences were tried, and these were often punished by fines which went into the lord's pocket. The common offences included poaching a neighbour's strip of land during ploughing. As the strips were separated only by a furrow between the ridges, it was obviously not always an intentional encroachment, when driving a team of oxen along a narrow demarcation, and it was in everyone's interests to settle such disputes amicably.

More important offences against public order were punished by those instruments of justice which we now find so 'quaint' – stocks, whipping-posts, pillory, ducking-stool and, of course, gallows. A hundred or shire court held, as was customary, in the open air in 1124 was presided over by Ralph Basset, lord of the manor of Sapcote in Leicestershire, who may have been the King's sheriff in the county, or possibly he was the first Justiciar of All England, appointed by the King, Henry I, to travel to all parts of the country and hear important cases as the King's representative. At any rate, he did his duties zealously. The Anglo-Saxon Chronicle tells the grisly tale: 'In this same year, after St. Andrew's day before Christmas, Ralph Basset held a court of the king's thanes at Hundehoh in Leicestershire, and hanged there more thieves than ever before: forty-four of them in all were despatched in no time, and six had their eyes put out and were castrated. Many honest men said a great injustice had been done in executing many of them; but our Lord God

Almighty, from whom no secrets are hid, He sees the poor oppressed by every kind of injustice; first they are bereft of their property, and then they are slain.'

Basset's savagery was perhaps exceptional, but we should not be under the illusion that the growing age of chivalry, in which troubadours sang of romantic courtship in the great halls, and Geoffrey of Monmouth invented the 'legends' of King Arthur and his knights, had anything whatever to do with the ordinary peasants of the countryside. They suffered at the hands of the lords, and if they sought any comfort in religion, it was not usually with much help from the parish priest.

He was just as likely as the lord of the manor to be illiterate, and if he was not actually married, he probably kept a 'hearth-girl' who 'kindled his fire but extinguished his virtue'. Perhaps it was an error of psychological tactics for the Normans to make the parish priest responsible for keeping the parish bull, ram, boar and stallion. But if he ignored the rule of celibacy, he was zealous in some of his other duties, such as collecting the parish tithes. These were the profits the Church exacted from its meek and humble flock – one tenth of all their produce: crops, wool, lambs, milk, eggs and so on. The forgiveness of sins was doubtless in proportion to the size of the harvest.

Moral offences were usually tried by the ecclesiastical courts after the Conquest, except in so far as they impinged on the lord's rights, as they did, for instance, when 'leyrwite' was due. The lord of the manor was entitled to payment of a fine called 'merchet' when a serf's daughter was married (with the lord's permission). If she lost her virginity before she was married, however, the lord could exact the fine called 'leyrwite'. This was because a *legitimate* child was part of the manorial property, but an *illegitimate* one was not and so represented a loss to the lord, a bastard being deemed outside the law and a free man. Thus at Halesowen, Worcestershire, the daughter of William of Liche was fined twelve pence for fornication in 1270; and at Wakefield, Yorkshire, in 1316, Juliana Sibbson was fined two shillings for being deflowered before she was married and for being married without licence. The lords were not willing to see the Church profit by their losses. Thus at Ramsey manor in Huntingdonshire John Marsh, who persisted in committing adultery with Sarah the wife of Simon Hewen and was repeatedly fined by the church court, had to be handed over to the lord of the manor and put in the stocks instead. It cannot have been easy for unmarried peasant lovers to exercise their passion in those days. They must have made love in the open, in woods or cornfields, and the only evidence of it for the courts, apart from malicious or jealous tell-tales, was obvious pregnancy.

This was the social background against which we must see the oldest surviving manor houses, which date from the middle of the twelfth century. There are two reasons why this period provides the earliest examples to remain. The first is that by this time they were usually being built of stone rather than timber. The second is that Henry II accelerated the incidence of manor-house building by eliminating unlicensed castles after the anarchy and inter-baronial warfare of Stephen's reign and allowed only royal castles to be entrusted to men who could be depended on to maintain the peace.

The tensions of a conquered nation were beginning to abate, and both lords and vassals were learning to consider their domestic welfare with a little more knowledge from increasing literacy. The growth of the common law made it important for a man to know his rights, as freeman or serf, and the professional soldier thought of war in terms of foreign conquest rather than civil strife.

A case which came before the lord of the manor at Wakefield in 1286 illustrates the point. The brothers Robert and John, sons of Thomas of Wakefield, both claimed to be his rightful heir. John disputed Robert's claim because, although Robert was the elder, he had been born before his parents were married. But Robert said that his parents had plighted their troth before he was born, and it was the custom in those parts for the elder brother to be heir as long as he was born after plight-troth. The lord granted his claim. Custom played an important role in questions of rights, even in Edward I's days.

The classic form of manor house which was being established around this time was centred upon the hall, which might be on the ground floor and aisled by pillars which supported its high roof, or on an upper floor which had below it an undercroft used for storage purposes, or for the servants, or even for harbouring livestock. The floor of the hall would be of earth if it was on the ground floor, strewn with rushes and with a central hearth. The roof would be thatched, and the windows closed with wooden shutters. Bede says that Abbot Benedict 'sent messengers to Gaul to fetch makers of glass . . . who were at that time unknown in Britain', that they might glaze the windows of his church, with the cloisters and dining-rooms. This was at Monkwearmouth, near Sunderland, in the seventh century, but it was

Stokesay Castle, Shropshire. The fine timber roof of the great hall on the first floor

to be a long number of years before it became a common practice to glaze the windows of ordinary houses.

At the end of the great hall where the lord and his family dined, often at a table on a raised dais and usually referred to as the 'high table' end of the hall, there would be a solarium or 'solar', the private apartment of the lord's family. It might have a lavatory, or 'garderobe', built on to it, and there might be a domestic chapel, too. At the opposite end of the hall, particularly a ground-floor one, it was common to have three doors which led into kitchen, buttery and pantry. The main doorway into the hall would be in a side wall near this end, and often another door directly opposite – what we would now call the back door – led into a courtyard, where the household drew its water supply from a well. To screen all these doorways from the hall and prevent draughts, it became common to place wooden screens across and later to build a permanent structure for this purpose. The area thus resulting between the screen and the service doorways is known as the 'screens passage'.

We might regard this as the basic blueprint for the medieval manor house, and although there were many variations on the theme, as we shall see, the concept of a house in which the hall was the central and dominant feature and, as it were, the only 'living-room', was not to change for a very long time.

The great hall was where the lord of the manor would usually hold court as he travelled round his various manors to maintain his estates and administer justice. Even today, one can detect a slight feeling of awe in some older country folk when they refer to their village's 'big house', the inside of which they have never seen; and in Norman times, the only occasion on which any of the village peasants would have seen inside the lord's house was if they were brought before the manorial court for some misdemeanour. It must have been a highly intimidating occasion for them, leaving their hovels and entering the lord's great hall, so magnificent and well built, like an enormous barn, where the lord and his bailiff were seated at the high table, like judges in a modern courtroom, with a huge coloured tapestry hanging behind them, and witnesses waiting to give evidence and staring at them as they were brought in, while all the lord's household staff probably still lingered in the background.

If the hall were an aisled one, the reason was to solve the practical problem of roofing a hall of such width. The roof timbers used were exclusively of oak, and the aisle pillars supported junctions of the relatively short timbers that were generally available, whilst the height of the roof, such a distinctive feature of the older manor houses, was necessitated by the need for smoke from the central hearth to rise and escape through it. As medieval carpentry became more skilled and wall fireplaces were introduced, so the great hall roof became progressively lower and lost its need for aisles with their obstructive pillars.

Ightham Mote, Kent, looking towards the outer courtyard

CHAPTER 2

The Oldest Survivals

There are several difficulties about the manor houses to be included in this chapter, which will not occur in later chapters. Many fragments of Norman buildings, which may have been built as manor houses, can still be found – an arched doorway here, an undercroft there – but which do not show us anything of what the complete house was like, and of whose history we know nothing. It has often been almost entirely demolished to make way for a more modern building. And even among those survivals which are more than fragmentary, one cannot always be certain whether the building was actually a manor house when it was erected, even if it is called one now. Whatever else may remain of a *possible* medieval manor house, the crucial survival is the great hall. However much it may have been restored, modernized or otherwise changed, a manor house with a proven great hall of pre-fifteenth-century date is an architectural treasure, but there are not many of them left now. A house built primarily for comfortable living rather than for keeping out the enemy was not built as strong and as solid as those manor houses which are so often called castles, and it is not surprising that so few of them have been kept in anything like their original form throughout the centuries. We can count it as a matter of pure luck that a small number of them have, for no one in the Middle Ages or in Tudor times, when so much rebuilding was being done, consciously looked at a manor house and said, 'This must be preserved for posterity.'

One or two particularly old and impressive survivals have been included here even when the hall no longer exists, but generally speaking, I shall allow the existence of a hall to dictate which buildings may reasonably be described as surviving manor houses of the early Middle Ages. It will be noticed that a high proportion of the oldest ones fall in that area of England which is traversed by the Jurassic limestone, for when building in stone began, this was the most easily quarried and worked stone available. Thus from the coast of Dorset, through Somerset and the Cotswolds, the east Midlands, and through Lincolnshire up to north Yorkshire, manor-house builders substituted stone for timber earlier than those in most other parts of the country.

Among the earliest surviving great halls in England is the so-called Oakham Castle in Leicestershire. It was not really a castle but a manor house which was later fortified under royal licence. The hall is the only part that remains, but it is a superb example of the aisled hall discussed in the previous chapter and deserves examination. It was built *c*.1180–90.

The castle site, reached now from the market-place of Rutland's former county town, was surrounded by earthworks when the manor was owned by the Anglo-Saxon Queen Eadgyth, wife of Edward the Confessor. Domesday Book records that the town was still Crown property after the Conquest, but by 1130 the manor had been granted to the powerful local Ferrers family. The hall was built by Walkelyn de Ferriere, and probably at the same time a surrounding moat and curtain wall were constructed.

The hall is not quite of the classic medieval pattern. The stone piers forming the aisles of four bays do not support a single overall roof, but the roofs of the aisles are of lean-to construction, not quite reaching the eaves of the central roof over the 'nave'. The foliage capitals of the circular pillars are so well carved, and so similar to those in the chancel of Canterbury Cathedral, that it is generally assumed they are the work of the same craftsman, William of Sens, or one of his men, and it is by this work that the building is dated. There are also fine stone carvings of animals and musicians. The entrance to the hall was originally at one end, but this has been re-sited during restoration to the centre of the 'front' wall. The three doorways which once led to kitchen, buttery and pantry can still be seen.

The most famous thing about Oakham Castle today is its collection of horseshoes. They hang round the walls of the hall – horseshoes of all sizes, some made of wood and some rusting with age – the most splendid collection of good-luck symbols exacted by long tradition from peers of the realm when passing through the town. There is one from Elizabeth I and one from Elizabeth II. Tradition has it that the custom began with the hall's builder, whose name gives the clue. His ancestor can hardly have been William the Conqueror's blacksmith, as 'farrier' implies, but he was Master of the King's Horse, and it is said that if any peer defaulted in presenting the requisite

Oakham Castle, Leicestershire – the great hall

horseshoe, the town had the right to remove one from his horse. George V failed to pay the toll, but by his time monarchs had given up riding round the country on horses, so he was not penalized.

An earlier single-storey hall, built around 1140 as a prebendal manor house, survives at Horton Court, Avon, standing beside the church in this village at the southern end of the Cotswolds near Chipping Sodbury. Only the north wing of the present house is Norman, the rest being of Tudor or later date. The hall has one entrance opposite the priest's doorway of the church, and another on the opposite side, as was customary, and this is one of the few completely defenceless manor houses surviving from the Norman period. The hall is a tall stone building, but the roof is not the original one.

The manor house at Hemingford Grey, Cambridgeshire, claims to be the oldest inhabited house in England, but Penfound Manor, near Poundstock in Cornwall, certainly beats it, since it has a thick Saxon wall in its structure and was once owned by Edward the Confessor's wife, the same Eadgyth who held Oakham Castle. Most of the present house, however, is Elizabethan or later. Hemingford's other chief rival to the claim must be Saltford, between Bristol and Bath. Though its main structure now is seventeenth century, its hall is on the upper floor and may date from as early as 1150. There is a lion carved in stone on one of the gables, ancient wall painting has been traced there, and one of the hall's two-light windows has a stone window-seat, as well as typical Norman decoration outside. The building looks rather like a barn from a distance, and indeed, it is now in use as a farmhouse.

The ruins of a manor house at Portslade, near Brighton, are of similar date. Apparently the twelfth-century ruins, in the grounds of a convent, were more extensive at the beginning of the nineteenth century, but the stone of the real ruin was pillaged to build a sham one not far away.

The grounds of Hemingford Grey's manor house are bordered by the River Ouse on one side and a moat encloses the rest. Much alteration has taken place here, but the original Norman house plan is still recognizable. It is a two-storey building of limestone with the hall and a bedroom over the ground-floor store-room and domestic offices. It was built around 1160 by Payne de Hemingford. An outside staircase led to the upper floor – the doorway has since been changed to a window, but it was in the end wall, near the angle, and not in the side wall as

Hemingford Manor, Cambridgeshire – the fireplace in the hall

was more usual. Norman two-light windows remain in some of the walls, and the original chimney-piece is flanked by columns with carved capitals.

The idea of the chimney was only beginning to gain acceptance in England at about this time, having been introduced from Italy, and this is therefore among the country's earliest examples. The wide apertures of early chimneys allowed down-draughts to fill the rooms with smoke, but the innovation was clearly an improvement on the open hearth in the centre of the floor. Chimneys naturally made their appearance first on upper floors.

It is hardly surprising that through eight centuries this ancient house has undergone a great deal of change, particularly in the Tudor period, but sympathetic restoration has been carried out, and this perhaps gives Hemingford Manor the right to be regarded as the oldest complete manor house remaining in England. It shows clearly the growing tendency at the time for men of wealth and power to start looking to their comforts and good living rather than to defence.

For a short time in the eighteenth century, the house was the home of two famous sisters, Maria and Elizabeth Gunning, the daughters of John Gunning, an Irish squire. They were celebrated for their beauty – 'the handsomest women alive' according to Horace Walpole. They were married in the same year, Maria to the Earl of Coventry and Elizabeth, one year her junior, to the Duke of Hamilton. But fortune did not smile on the girls for long. Elizabeth was widowed after six years of marriage, and two years later Maria died at the age of twenty-seven, apparently from lead poisoning in her cosmetics.

Burton Agnes, in Humberside, has two manor houses side by side, and the more modern one, being a fairly spectacular Jacobean mansion, tends to distract attention from the modest brick building which is its neighbour. But the brick hides an upper-floor hall built around 1170 with a vaulted undercroft below. The undercroft, this time, is aisled, by one row of columns with carved capitals. A newel stair leads from it up to the hall. These narrow spiral stairs were always made to be mounted in a clockwise direction, the theory apparently being that if raiders had penetrated the ground floor, the retreating occupier had room to manœuvre his sword arm and was in a good position to fight off his attackers – always assuming, of course, that he was right-handed. Since the new manor house was built here, the old has been used as servants' quarters and as a laundry, and its roof had to be replaced long ago. Behind the building a shed houses the well and the donkey-wheel by which water was raised.

Appleton Manor, formerly in Berkshire, now in Oxfordshire, has been called by Sir Nikolaus Pevsner 'an amazing survival' with a doorway 'worthy of any major church'. The single-storey house dates from about 1190, and the doorway in question is Norman round-arched work with three orders of colonnettes and deep moulding round the arches. Inside there are also two round-arched doors which led from the hall to the service rooms.

The old manor house at Sutton Courtenay, on the other side of Abingdon and, like Appleton, a recent acquisition of the county from Berkshire, was also built between 1190 and 1200. It is known as Norman Hall and should not be confused with the Jacobean manor house nearby, which also has ancient origins, though not much in evidence. Norman Hall is a simpler rectangular building of stone, with lancet windows in the ground-floor hall. The place has also been known in its time as Court House and Manor Farm, all of which goes to show its versatility,

The manor house at Sutton Courtenay, Oxfordshire

if not its appreciation, over the centuries. It is possible that it was originally the chapel of the manor house built here by Reginald Courtenay, who was granted the manor by Henry II and whose descendants evidently started building their new manor house before a century had passed.

Swanborough Manor in East Sussex is of similar date. This had a circular window in the gable. As so often, however, later owners' alterations included dividing the hall horizontally into two rooms, as well as adding chimneys and a chapel, so that little original work remains, as is the case at Hambledon in Hampshire, where the thirteenth-century manor house – now a farmhouse – had an upper-floor hall with square-headed windows and an arcaded undercroft, and what was probably a domestic chapel was added to the hall, like the chancel to the nave of a church.

At the village of Boothby Pagnell, near Grantham in Lincolnshire, the remarkable preservation of a small Norman manor house in the grounds of the modern Hall is another exception to the general rule that castles did not give way to manor houses

Boothby Pagnell, Lincolnshire. The thirteenth-century manor house

until the end of the thirteenth century. This one was defended to the extent of having a moat round it and having its living-quarters, as so often in this period, on the first floor. From the outside it looks simple, though not by any means primitive. It was built about 1200 with a hall and solar above the ground floor, reached by an outside staircase and a round-arched doorway in the side wall near the angle with the end wall. The stairway was, unusually, at right angles to the wall, not parallel with it. The material used for the building was the local Jurassic limestone rubble, and the walls are four feet thick in places. The roof is not the original one, nor are some of the windows, but the general style of this Romanesque house is perfectly clear. One round-arched window has a stone window-seat built into it. The ground floor is rib-vaulted and separated into two parts like the hall and solar above, the ground-floor dividing wall clearly having been built for its load-bearing function. The hall has a fireplace, the chimney being step-buttressed.

Charlestone Manor, in East Sussex, lies near the secluded village of Westdean on the South Downs. This also is a moated site, and the south wing is contemporary with Boothby Pagnell, consisting of two storeys with the hall above. William the Conqueror's cup-bearer was the lord of the manor at the time of the Domesday survey, when it was called Cerlestone. There is a fine Romanesque window in one end wall, and the property also includes a medieval dovecote and an early tithe barn. The larger part of this house, however, consists of Tudor and Georgian extensions.

The muddy creek village of West Wittering, below the other end of the Downs, has Cakeham Manor, which also displays mainly Tudor and Georgian architecture, but part of an early thirteenth-century hall and undercroft remains, built in stone, whereas the fortified extension, built in the sixteenth century, is of brick. At this time the house belonged to the bishops of Chichester, whose rabbits devoured the wheat grown in the fields and were a cause of complaint by the farmers. Rabbits had been introduced into England from Europe not long before, for their meat and skins. The licence to crenellate at Cakeham had been granted in 1447, but the building was in ruins then, and the Tudor house was started more or less from scratch.

The lords in the arable farming areas of southern and eastern England had their peasants marling and manuring the land each year to increase its yield. Sheep dung and farmyard manure were used, as well as lime, but the dung was naturally scarce in arable regions, and the lord's courtyard was sometimes used as a repository from where it was collected in carts by the peasants for distribution in the fields.

In ruins now is the ancient manor house of flint at Warnford, near West Meon, Hampshire. It is known as King John's House by that once common attribution of otherwise unaccountable bridges and earthworks to the devil and otherwise unaccountable mansions and castles to the king (thought by many to be the devil's confederate). In Warnford's case, however, there is greater excuse for the error, since the lord of the manor changed his name to St John after his father had been outlawed for trying to assassinate Henry II. The hall here was of the aisled ground-floor type, divided by four pillars, some of which are alleged to have been reduced to rubble by the ivy clinging to them. The entrance at the south-west corner led into a screens passage with the service rooms off to the left, and opposite the entrance was the stairway leading to the solar above.

Several manor houses survive from the middle of the thir-teenth century, without having any great interest except to the

Charney Bassett Manor, Oxfordshire

architectural specialist. Cogges Manor, near Witney, Oxfordshire, Lodsworth Manor and the ruins of Crowhurst Manor in
Sussex, both two-storeyed, date from this period, as does Charney Bassett Manor, originally in Berkshire but now in Oxfordshire.

Much more interesting is Luddesdown Court, near Cobham
in Kent. This manor house of flint has very early origins. Cut in
the plaster of one wall is the outline of a ship, and a wall fireplace
in the first-floor hall is one of the earliest surviving examples.
The solar forms an L-shape with the hall, and the house generally seems to be of around 1230, though it may well be earlier and
claims to be the oldest house in England still in use. That is of
course very doubtful. The lord of the manor here in 1346 was one
of Edward III's officers when the King besieged Calais, and
nearly a century afterwards the owner was Thomas de Montacute, seventh Earl of Salisbury, who died during the siege of
Orleans. The house had a bear-pit and a dovecote – or, to be
more accurate, a pigeon-loft. Only the lord of the manor was
permitted to build a dovecote, required mainly for the purpose

of supplying his table with fresh meat during the lean winter and spring months, though pigeon's eggs became a fashionable delicacy, too.

The lord's pigeons can hardly have been appreciated by the peasant farmers any more than they loved the bishop's rabbits, for the feathered inhabitants of a sizeable cote would have fed off the tenants' crops and gorged a fair weight of valuable grain each year. By the Stuart period, there were reckoned to be more than twenty-five thousand dovecotes in England, and the largest ones had nesting holes for a thousand pairs of doves. The guano was sometimes used for manuring the fields when sheep dung was in short supply.

Barnston Manor at Church Knowle, Dorset, is now a stylish farmhouse, in splendid rural isolation, with stone roof tiles. It was originally built of Purbeck limestone around 1260 and is one of the places where we can trace English ownership after the Conquest, since its name comes from Bern, a Saxon lord of the manor. In Elizabethan times it was the property of the Clavell family whose monuments are in the church, and it was no doubt they who gave the front of the house its beauty treatment, with mullioned, transomed and latticed windows, and reduced the ceiling height of the unaisled great hall behind the façade. A two-storeyed wing with solar above was built across the west end of the hall, forming a T-shaped house, and the solar had a window-seat, rebates for the window shutters, and slots for the shutter bolts.

Chingle Hall, at Goosnargh in Lancashire, is supposed to have been built by Adam de Singleton in 1260, though there is precious little visible evidence for that now except for the original front door of tarred oak. The house is better known today for the doubtful distinction of being the most haunted house in Britain (though there is a strong rival claimant in Dorset). In a county more prone to gullibility than most, that is perhaps not surprising when we remember that the Catholic hero St John Wall was born here and that his severed head was venerated as a holy relic after his execution at Worcester in 1679.

Not far from the south coast, north-west of Lulworth, is the village of Owermoigne, where one of Dorset's oldest houses remains within its moated site amid modern development which the lord of the manor who built it in 1270 could never have seen in his wildest medieval dreams. The house has elegant Early English traceried windows in the wall of its upper-floor hall, and there are rebates for the shutters as well as

The old stone manor house at Donington-le-Heath, Leicestershire, which was originally moated

stone window-seats. Much of the original house has disappeared, but it is clear that the hall was reached by an outside staircase.

At the tiny village of Donington-le-Heath, right at the centre of the Leicestershire coalfield near Coalville, a small stone-built manor house of about 1280 is the county's oldest surviving house. The hall was on the first floor, reached by a staircase which has disappeared – possibly it was a timber one. This is a very solid-looking building, which is not surprising, as it was built of Charnwood Forest granite, a very hard and difficult material to work. The architecture is therefore plain and unornamented, but from the outside the interest lies in the buttresses at the corners and in some pointed windows, heralding the Gothic style in local domestic architecture. We do not know as much as we would like to about this house's history, but coal was already being mined in the vicinity when it was built, and it may be that the hamlet, like several coalfield towns and villages, had its origins in this industrial development. Some alterations

The surviving chapel of Old Soar Manor, Kent

were made to this house in the Tudor period, and more recently it was in use as a farmhouse, then as a pigsty, but the property was acquired by the County Council and restored and is now used as a museum – one of the county's most valuable preservations.

Old Soar Manor, near Sevenoaks, Kent, in an area rich in manorial estates, is also of the late thirteenth century, though a later large farmhouse comprises the major part of this building. Only the stone-built solar, with a garderobe and a tiny chapel, survives, reached by a circular stone stair now within the Georgian farmhouse. The upper floor here was supported on large blocks of stone. The chapel had a glazed window and could be reached by its own stairway to avoid disturbing the occupants of the solar.

The Old Hall at West Bromwich was built around the same time, with an aisled ground-floor hall. The early lords of the manor were successively of the Devereux, Marnham and Stanley families, and the property was kept up by its later owners until the eighteenth century. Then at some time the hall became

The former manor house at Meare, Somerset

incorporated in a row of tenement houses and was forgotten until 1950. The derelict tenements were awaiting demolition when the old hall was rediscovered, and the enterprising local council saved and restored it, and it is now in use as a restaurant – too much restored to bear much resemblance to the medieval great hall, but an interesting survival, none the less, with its old moat re-excavated and an Elizabethan gatehouse leading to the courtyard and the great hall.

Further east, Little Chesterford, near Saffron Walden, Essex, has a manor house with a timber aisled hall and solar wing of the late thirteenth century. Much alteration went on here in the Elizabethan period, including the division of the hall into two floors, and the place is now a farmhouse, as is the manor house of similar date at Meare, in Somerset. This one, however, was owned by the Abbot of Glastonbury, and it was built of stone with traceried Gothic windows and a hall on the first floor, though this area was peaceful enough. It had a large fireplace in the room below the hall, which must have been either the kitchen or the servants' room, with the solar (unusually, in this case, larger than the hall) in a wing forming an L-shaped building.

Those manor houses which were not provided with a moat usually had a fish pond, for there were obligatory fish days on Wednesdays and Fridays, even outside the monasteries. In 1283 at Worcester, the steward and a servant of Sir Henry Hubart and the reeve of Hilberworth were cited for not observing the fasts and eating meat 'contrary to the warning of the parish priest'. Meare, however, stood beside a lake (which was drained in the eighteenth century). At the same time as he built the house, the Abbot, Adam de Sodbury, built a Fish House beside the lake, where fish caught in the mere were salted and stored by the retainer who lived there, until they were required for the manor house table.

Fish would have been on the menu twice a week at Norbury Manor in Derbyshire, for the manor belonged to the long-suffering Catholic family of Fitzherbert. It was Sir Henry, the fifth Baron Norbury, who built the original house here at the beginning of the fourteenth century, although it is now buried within a brick mansion of more than four hundred years later. The hall faces the churchyard, and the church contains several fine old monuments to the family, including the thirteenth baron, Sir Anthony, the judge and author of a *Boke of Husbandry*, who died in 1538.

What remains of the manor house beside the church at Yardley Hastings, in Northamptonshire, dates from around 1320, and as the village name tells us, it was a manor of the powerful Hastings family. This had a ground-floor hall with a screens passage and service rooms, and above them, a solar, bedchamber and garderobe. At the high table end of the great hall the lord and his family dined on a dais, which became a common enough custom in the days when the earth floors were strewn with straw or rushes, not without reason, for Erasmus of Rotterdam referred in his correspondence to English house floors, 'strewed with rushes, beneath which lies an ancient collection of beer, grease, fragments, bones, spittle, excrement of dogs and cats, and everything that is nasty'. Although carpets had been introduced from Spain by Eleanor of Castile in the mid-thirteenth century, bare floors persisted in England until the sixteenth century.

Northborough in Cambridgeshire has another fortunate survivor from the early fourteenth century. The manor house here is mainly a Jacobean rebuilding, but the medieval gateway and ground-floor unaisled hall remain more or less intact. The house has a fine decorated original chimney, of hexagonal shape, with gables, finials, animal heads and battlemented top. An unusual right-angle turn was made in the staircase leading up to the solar. The village is near Peterborough, and the house was built around 1330–40 by the lord of the manor, Geoffrey de la Marn. In the sixteenth century, the property passed to the Claypole family. John Claypole was one of those who joined John Hampden in refusing to pay Ship Money to Charles I, and Cromwell not only made him a baronet but married his favourite daughter, Elizabeth, to Claypole's son. It was the death of Elizabeth in 1658 that led directly to Cromwell's own breakdown and death, and the Lord Protector's widow lived in this house until her death.

Back across the border into Northamptonshire, near Oundle, is Southwick Hall, the ancient seat of the Knyvets and then the Lymes who married into the family in the fifteenth century. Parts of this stone building date from early in the fourteenth century, one of the upper rooms in a tower-like wing having been in use then as a chapel. Some of the building here was done, as was part of the parish church, by Sir John Knyvet, who was a Chancellor of England. Extensions and alterations were carried out in the Elizabethan period, and the much gabled, mullioned and chimneyed face the house presents now is mainly of that cosmetic age, but some original work remains in what was, under Edward I, a relatively peaceful part of the country.

Mancetter Hall in Warwickshire was built during the reign of Edward III and is a timber-framed house with an aisled ground-floor hall and a projecting wing with service rooms and solar above. Like so many lofty old halls, this one was later given a false ceiling to create another floor above. It forms an attractive group with its gazebos and the nearby church above the village green, but it is a place of tragedy, for when Mary Tudor came to the throne, it was the home of George Glover, one of the Protestant martyrs who was put to death in Coventry.

Little survives, either, of the original Creslow Manor House in Buckinghamshire, built around 1330 with a great hall, solar, tower, crypt and detached chapel. The manor belonged to the Knights Hospitallers in the sixteenth century, i.e. before the Dissolution, but later declined into a farmhouse, not surprisingly, perhaps, since Creslow had long been a famous pasture area for royal herds of cattle.

Clevedon Court, on the Bristol Channel coast, has been called 'one of the most valuable relics of domestic architecture in

England'. The central and chief medieval structure of this building dates from early in the fourteenth century, but there are parts which are even earlier. The great hall, kitchen and porch are original stone-built remains from the reign of Edward II. The porch is buttressed and is entered through a Gothic arch, and it has a portcullis in it, operated by a windlass in the room above when it was partly fortified. Flanking the upper porch is a small overhanging room believed to have been the original chapel, with square-headed windows and reticulated tracery. A newel stairway leads to this from the hall, which has a transomed window of four lights and a round arch, and a squint permitted a view of the hall from the chapel. The hall is panelled in oak now, and the eighteenth-century owner, Sir Abraham Elton, reduced its height to put in another floor above it. A porch at the back of the house originally led to a courtyard, where some defensive walls remain with a tower possibly as old as the twelfth century.

The Elton family made Clevedon Court even more famous for its literary connections than the medieval lords of the manor made it with their building works. Arthur Hallam, nephew of Sir Charles Elton, inspired Tennyson's finest work, *In Memoriam*, but the poet did not know Clevedon Court. The house had undergone much alteration and extension by the time Thackeray became a frequent guest and wrote part of *Vanity Fair* here. He later portrayed the house as 'Castlewood' in *Henry Esmond*, though the setting of the novel is Hampshire, but part of the house was burnt down in 1882 and one wing had to be rebuilt. It was a good place for a writer, at any rate, set well out to the east of the town, which was, at that time, bigger than Weston-super-Mare, and unusually far from the church of the medieval manor. Not many years before Thackeray arrived there, it had been called 'a residence fitting for the Prince of Hermits'. Alas, it is no longer so, for the Bristol road roars by it, and the M5 motorway makes its presence heard.

Forty miles north-east in the Gloucestershire Cotswolds is Daneway House at Sapperton, the oldest parts of which date from before 1339, when the lord of the manor, Henry de Clifford, was given licence to celebrate Mass there. The ground-floor hall had a central hearth and at one end a solar, the chapel being built as an extension near the entrance. The roof timbers of the original hall, which was made into two floors by the Hancox family who owned the house from 1397 to 1860, were blackened by the smoke from the hearth.

The most famous period of Daneway's story came as recently

as 1903, however, when it was owned by Lord Bathurst, who lent it to the William Morris-inspired furniture-maker Ernest Gimson and his group of craftsmen. One of his colleagues, Edward Barnsley, restored Daneway House, and it was then used as a showroom for the furniture made in the outbuilding workshops.

Hidden away in the Oxfordshire Chilterns not far from Henley-on-Thames is Stonor Park, the ancestral home of the Stonor family whose heads became the Barons Camoys after one of their number went to France with Henry V and led the left wing at Agincourt. The Stonor family have been here since the twelfth century, and John Leland described their house in his time as 'byldyd with tymber, brike and flinte'. The fifteenth-century brickwork is among the earliest in the region, but among this and the Tudor and later building on the site are some thirteenth- and fourteenth-century remains which qualify the house for a place in this chapter. Sir Richard de Stonor built the original great hall and solar towards the end of the thirteenth century. Part of it was pulled down later, probably during the following century when Sir John de Stonor enlarged the house and built a new timber-framed hall with a buttery and pantry off. The roof of this hall remains, though everything else has been modernized. The Stonors also built a private chapel which was enlarged in 1349, and this also has since been greatly remodelled, so that the medieval manor is now, to say the least, obscure. There was also a dwelling for six priests, which has totally disappeared.

What Pevsner calls the 'haphazard growth' of the house applies equally to the manor, for it was scattered about neighbouring parishes in the thirteenth century as the Stonors grew in power and influence and bought widely dispersed lands. Sir John de Stonor was Chief Justice of Common Pleas under Edward III, but the year in which so much rebuilding was done here was the year of the Black Death. The chief family commercial interest was in wool, not here in the beech-clad Chilterns but in the sheep-runs of their West Country manors. They would not therefore have felt the disastrous effects of the plague so much as those who relied totally on arable farming, and their wealth and good living are indicated by the presence of two companies of players at the house during Sir Thomas Stonor's Christmas festivities in 1482. A few years before, Thomas Betson, a wool merchant betrothed to a ward of Lord Camoys, had written to her at Stonor from Calais. She was twelve. 'Be a good

eater of your meat alway, that ye may wax and grow fast to be a
woman. . . . And Allmighty Jesus make you a good woman and
send you always many good years and long to live in health and
virtue to his pleasure.' It was a period when the English upper
classes, not only literate now but well educated too, were
beginning the fashion of letter-writing which has told us so
much about the social history of the times. Betson married his
fiancée when she was fifteen.

In this house is the room in which Dame Cecilia Stonor gave
refuge to the Jesuit priest Edmund Campion, in the Elizabethan
period of religious persecution. He set up a secret printing-press
here in 1580, in order to print attacks on the Protestants and
boost the morale of the persecuted Catholics. His *Ten Reasons
Against the Anglican Church* helped to make him the scapegoat in
Elizabeth's propaganda to keep England free of 'Roman tyranny', and he was arrested, tortured on the rack, hanged,
drawn and quartered for alleged seditious conspiracy, the
Jesuits having been identified as the shock troops of a supposed
Catholic take-over. An Act of Parliament in the same year
increased penalties against ordinary recusants, and hearing
Mass could be punished by a fine of a hundred marks and twelve
months in prison. John Stonor was himself arrested in this house
and taken to the Tower in August 1581, soon after Campion's
arrest in Berkshire.

Stonor House stands peacefully now in what Pope called its
'gloomy verdure' – amid the folds of the well-wooded hills and
in a romantic deer park which has never been subjected to the
prettifying designs of such as 'Capability' Brown.

Perhaps the most picturesque of all the earliest surviving
manor houses, externally, is Ightham Mote, near Sevenoaks in
Kent. Some of the fabric of this moated manor house dates from
the twelfth century, but it was in the first half of the fourteenth
that the great hall we see at present was built in stone to replace
an earlier timber house on the site – the name of the house comes
from 'moot' – a medieval meeting-place or council which assem-
bled there. The house is built round a square cobbled courtyard
and surrounded by a moat crossed by a stone bridge leading
straight to the hall, which has remarkably neat trussed roof
rafters either side of a central stone arch. The original domestic
chapel, over a vaulted crypt, was replaced in the sixteenth
century by a new one reached by an outer staircase from the
courtyard. As well as the chapel, timber-framed building and
red roof tiles were added at later periods, making Ightham an

architectural jumble but a homely mixture which was unquestionably on the way to the age of comforts even when the stone walls were stood up to their knees in a marginally defensive moat.

Swans, doves and peacocks add to the romantic air of mediaeval well-being evoked by the stone walls, latticed windows, crenellated tower and heavy oak doors of this manor house beautifully situated in a wooded valley, but the picture is deceptive – the fourteenth-century house was not yet in the age when log fires and minstrels, roast sucking pigs and hawking parties were the order of the day and swords could be hung on the walls merely for decoration. True, the moat would not have protected this house from much except burglars, perhaps, but the only robber in Ightham's long history seems to have been Richard III, who expelled the owners, the Haut family, for no worse offence than being related to the Woodvilles. Richard Haut had been sheriff of Kent in 1478 and 1483 and had won jousting tournaments in the King's presence. The family recovered Ightham after the Battle of Bosworth but eventually sold it. The Selby family were later owners, and it was Lady Dorothy Selby who is said to have deciphered the letters giving a veiled, not to say illegible, warning of the Gunpowder Plot. She was also an accomplished needlewoman, whose monument in the church says:

> She was a Dorcas
> Whose curious needle turned th' abused stage
> Of this lewd world into a Golden Age.

Whether Dorothy Selby was actually buried in the church, however, is open to question. When workmen were carrying out restoration work on the house in the nineteenth century, they discovered a walled-up cupboard with a female skeleton inside, and legend has it that it was Lady Dorothy, buried alive by friends of the Gunpowder conspirators in revenge for her having warned her cousin Lord Monteagle of the plot.

At Durleigh, near Bridgwater, Somerset, West Bower Manor House was long known as Bower Farm, and it must surely have been one of the most spectacular farmhouses in England. It is not a large house now, but it is a most interesting one and is only part of a grander house of the fourteenth century. It has two polygonal towers flanking the entrance. They have conical roofs, grotesque heads all round and two-light transomed windows which include some original glass. As well as flowers and plants, the glass has the initials A and M in it. These belonged to

Ightham Mote, Kent – the gatehouse and moat

Sir Alexander Hody, who was executed for treason in the fifteenth century, and his wife Margaret Coker. The lords of the manor had a thatched dovecote with nine hundred nest holes. Much of the house's ancient history is obscure, but it belonged to the Seymours in Henry VIII's time, and it is sometimes said (wrongly) to have been the birthplace of Jane Seymour. After the Seymours came Halswells and Tyntes before it was reduced to a farmhouse, but it has been rescued from certain oblivion in recent years and stands with its unusual façade overlooking a modern lake.

In the fourteenth century, the eruption of large country houses and what we now call stately homes was still a long way off, but in some cases, these later vast mansions evolved from what were originally manor houses in the strict sense. One such famous case is Penshurst Place in Kent, which was built round the nucleus of a fourteenth-century feudal hall. Sir John de Pulteney, a wool merchant, acquired the manor of what was then called Penchester and built a new house on the existing site in 1341. This book is not the place to go into the subsequent story of what became the home of dukes and the birthplace of Sir Philip Sidney, but the great hall deserves its place here. It is not only the 'masterpiece of the whole house' but is easily the finest hall of its period in Britain. It is unaisled and, next to Oakham, the largest of the halls discussed in this chapter. The high roof is constructed of chestnut, and carved wooden figures round the walls are said to be the medieval owners' retainers. The windows have Gothic lights within round-arched stonework, whilst the medieval trestle tables are unique survivals. A solar, later converted into a state dining-room, adds to the Middle Ages fascination of this largely Tudor building, and from it, peepholes allowed its occupants to keep an eye on the servants in the hall.

Coming down to earth, as it were, we find the remains of another fourteenth-century manor house among the buildings of a large farm at Rockbourne, Hampshire. This, too, is a conglomeration of medieval and later buildings, but the hall of the original house remains with a thirteenth-century ground-floor chapel and a barn built at the same time as the house.

With few exceptions, there is a gap of some thirty years between the buildings of Penshurst and the next rural manor houses we can find. The reason is not hard to discover. A few years after the great hall at Penshurst was completed, rumours may have reached the English ports of a terrible calamity in the Far East. Travellers brought many tales to Europe of the mysterious Orient, which were doubtless listened to with the same curiosity but lack of personal involvement that most of us hear of a far-off disaster on television today. It is all a long way off. But within a couple of years, the disaster in distant Cathay had overtaken Europe and was sweeping through Britain. It was the Black Death. It is doubtful whether the country folk of England heard of this dread plague until it suddenly struck them down. No one escaped its horror. It killed lords and monks as impartially as it killed peasants and serfs, although the poor suffered most, as always. Sheep and oxen were wiped out as well as human beings. The after-effects of its appalling devastation were more acute in the country than in the towns. It had killed a third of the labour force. The soil lay neglected for want of men to till it, and houses stood half finished for want of men to build them.

Nevertheless, it is clear that, in spite of the death and disease all around them, the English peasantry carried on their normal way of life as well as they could, and even continued to pay to the lords of the manors the fines on inheritance occasioned by the deaths of relatives. But if the lords theoretically profited by land and livestock reverting to them when whole families were wiped out, they had to hire workers at higher wages to look after their ill-gotten gains.

Among the exceptions to the slump in building, possibly erected only seven years after the Black Death struck (although its exact date is not known), is Fiddleford Manor in Dorset, near Sturminster Newton. It may have been built for William Latimer, who in 1355 married Margaret Maury of Fiddleford and later became sheriff of Somerset and Dorset. Much reconstruction took place here in the sixteenth century, and the place eventually became a farmhouse, but part of the hall remains as well as the solar, and both are notable for their fine open timber roofs, with wind-braces and elaborately carved spandrels.

The Black Death lit a slow-burning fuse which exploded thirty years afterwards in the Peasants' Revolt, when Wat Tyler, John Ball and others led a rebellion against the lords' repression during the labour shortage, and against the wealth of the clergy, grown fat on tithes, and the poll tax imposed in 1381, among other injustices. The latter was the spark that fired the widespread riots. The tax was to pay for the King's wars in France, and the poorest peasant was expected to pay the same amount as the richest man in the kingdom – three groats.

The King and the barons promised reforms, including the

abolition of serfdom, but then suppressed the revolt by force, the fourteen-year-old King Richard telling the rebels: 'Serfs you are, and serfs you shall remain.' The revolt was broken, but any romantic notions of personal loyalty to one's lord that may have lingered from centuries ago were gone for ever. The lords of manors began to feel the pressures of labour relations, and labourers, like the knights before them, began to expect payment in money rather than in kind.

Among these lords were the Gawen family, who owned Alvediston in Wiltshire. A house called Norrington here began its life as their fourteenth-century manor house, built at the commencement of Richard II's reign, and it has a ground-floor hall of four bays, with an undercroft beneath the solar. A vaulted porch was added to this house in the following century, stone-built with a king's head on one of the corbels.

In Devon, the small village of Shute near Axminster sports a mainly Tudor house with one range dating from about 1380. It was built by the sheriff of Dorset and Somerset, Sir William Bonville. This was originally a tower house consisting of a first-floor hall with kitchen below, but in modern times another floor has been added between them. The hall has a fine roof with collar beams and curved wind-braces, and there is a huge fireplace in the kitchen. The hall is reached by a newel staircase between the old and new ranges and has interesting developments in medieval hygiene. Lavatory chambers were generally pushed out from the walls of the Norman houses, generally to be discharged into the moat and occasionally built with an elementary flushing system. Here, though their positions on either side of the fireplace might seem slightly perverse, they were serviced by channels in the walls. Privies may not have been referred to in polite conversation much, but in impolite conversation then, as now, they had alternative names, like 'jakes' and 'gong'. In royal and other great households which had a servant in charge of such conveniences, he was known, not unreasonably I suppose, as the 'groom of the stool' in later times.

Some additions were made to the original house at Shute by the fifteenth-century owner, Thomas Grey, Marquis of Dorset, who later built one of Britain's earliest country mansions of red brick at Bradgate Park in Leicestershire, where the nine days Queen was born. The Greys had acquired Shute through marriage with a daughter of the Bonville family. Subsequently it passed to the Poles, and in the eighteenth century, when the new house was built, much of the medieval work was demolished. Then the house became a girls' school, and finally it passed to the National Trust.

Further west near Totnes is one of the most dramatic and fascinating of medieval survivals in the south of England, Dartington Hall. It is perhaps also the best known, but not because of its medieval architecture. In 1925 the building was practically in ruins, but it was purchased, together with a large estate, and turned into the headquarters of what has been called 'an essay in the reconstruction of rural life'. The new lord of the manor, as it were, was Dr Leonard Elmhirst, a man much influenced, whilst working in Bengal, by Rabindranath Tagore and Mahatma Gandhi. He came here with his wealthy and idealistic American wife Dorothy, and together they developed the estate as an enlightened modern manor, with agriculture, weaving, forestry and other work, using the natural resources of a depressed area to provide local employment, education, crafts training and cultural activities for the workers and their families. Dartington Glass is the most famous outcome of this venture. But what of the medieval manor house?

It was built between 1388 and 1400 by a half-brother of Richard II, John Holland, Earl of Huntingdon and later Duke of Exeter. An earlier small manor house was incorporated in the building, and an early fourteenth-century barn remains nearby. The stone hall block and porch face a large quadrangle, and another later courtyard was originally a tilting yard. The newly fashion-conscious ladies in their embroidered gowns and wimples who watched the knights at jousting tournaments have been succeeded on the terrace by a more nonchalant figure – a Reclining Woman by Henry Moore. The vaulted porch has Richard II's arms on the central boss. The huge square kitchen has arched fireplaces fourteen feet high.

When the Elmhirsts bought Dartington, the great hall was open to the sky. It was given an oak hammer-beam roof in keeping with the period of its original construction, and a great deal of other restoration and careful remodelling went into the place, but it still has a fine medieval appearance from the main courtyard and must be counted among the most valuable remains of the period.

The National Trust owns what is perhaps one of the country's best-known domestic buildings of its date, the so-called Old Post Office at the coastal village of Tintagel, Cornwall. It is a tiny and late fourteenth-century manor house – a humble enough dwell-

Dartington Hall, Devon – the east front

ing, even for the time – with a hall and parlour, but the interior is no match for the outside of this fascinating building of local slate. The old roof soars and swoops like a fairground switchback, above shadowy and deceptive rough grey walls which look as though they might fall at any moment but have withstood all that the Atlantic forces could throw at them for five hundred years. They are between three and four feet thick in places. In the nineteenth century, the house was used as the district's letter-receiving office, and it is now restored and on view as such, but its medieval appearance is still easily discernible, the hall reaching up to the roof timbers which are of upper cruck construction, and the windows cut out of single blocks of stone.

One more survival from the late fourteenth century deserves mention here. The old manor house at Stanton Harcourt, in Oxfordshire, was almost entirely demolished in the eighteenth century, after the Harcourts, who had been here since the twelfth century, had finally left and the place had fallen into dereliction. But what was left has made the house famous – the kitchen and Pope's Tower. The spectacular medieval kitchen is the oldest part, the one remaining room of the house built by Thomas Harcourt, who died in 1417. The so-called Pope's Tower dates from about 1460 and was so named because Alexander Pope was a guest of Lord Harcourt here, when the house was already falling into ruin. He had his study at the top of the tower which had housed a priest on the floors below. Pope finished the fifth volume of his translation of Homer's *Iliad* here and in a letter to the Duke of Buckingham made fun of the huge kitchen: 'The horror of it has made such an impression on the country people that they believe the witches keep their Sabbath here, and that once a year the devil treats them with infernal venison, i.e. a toasted tiger stuffed with tenpenny nails.'

Joking apart, the kitchen *is* fairly awesome. It is over thirty feet square, with a high conical roof which was rebuilt in 1485. There are no chimneys in it. The smoke and steam were meant to escape through louvres, now gone. But that they did not entirely do so can be seen by the discoloration of the walls. The louvres could be turned according to the wind direction by climbing a newel staircase to a passage running inside the battlemented parapet round the roof. I should think the cooks found this too troublesome to bother with. On one wall are two fireplaces, and opposite are three ovens. One may look at the many tombs and effigies of the Harcourts in the village church and feel confident that, whatever else the lords of the manor did here, they must have been well fed.

CHAPTER 3

Watchful Barons

After the demolition of unlicensed castles by Henry II, and the consequent increase in the building of manor houses, barons in certain parts of England at different times had good reasons to defend their homes against attack, and many lords were given licence by the King to fortify their manor houses. The earliest recorded licences to crenellate were issued during the reign of King John, himself a great builder of both castles and manor houses. The chief threats to security, however, were to come later, from the Scots in the north, the Welsh in the west, and the French in the south.

One of the earliest substantial fortified manor houses that we know quite a bit about is Stokesay Castle in Shropshire. It is among the earliest in Britain and the best preserved of its kind, although if farmers had not used it badly in more recent times, storing grain in the cellar and making barrels in the hall, it might be in an even better state today. It stands in quiet countryside and has a serene appearance from across the millpond on its west side, but it is a constant wonder that it could have been built originally without fortifications in the thirteenth century with such open aspect within a few miles of the Welsh border, at a time when the Marcher lords and their knights slept with their hands on their swords, only too conscious of the fact that the marauding Celts of Llewellyn the Great not only kept a welcome in the hillsides but were apt to bring it across the border in the form of siege or ambush. The original manor house had a moat round it, now dry, but this would scarcely have deterred hostile forces from making life very unpleasant for the occupants.

The north tower dates from about 1240 and was built by the de Saye family who gave the hamlet, otherwise known as South Stoke, their name – Stoke de Saye. They had occupied the land since 1105. They and their successors must have been blessed with profound faith or supreme optimism – perhaps the former, for the de Sayes also rebuilt the church, and one of their successors as lord of the manor, John de Verdon, left Stokesay in

Sizergh Castle, Cumbria – the pele tower

Stokesay Castle, Shropshire

1290 to go on a crusade. The manor was then bought by Laurence de Ludlow, a wealthy wool merchant, who was evidently more pessimistic, for he obtained a licence to crenellate from Edward I in 1291. His successors lived at Stokesay for three centuries.

When Henry James visited Stokesay, he 'lay on the grass beside the well in the sunny court of this small castle and lazily appreciated the still definite details of medieval life'. And it is true that the remarkable state of preservation does present with the utmost clarity the conditions in which a well-to-do medieval family lived.

From the south, with its solid tower and castellated walls, the place, built of the local greeny-yellow sandstone, looks like a considerable fortress, but from the north it takes on the appearance of a castle from Grimm's fairy tales, for a half-timbered overhanging upper storey was added to its north tower during Laurence's rebuilding. The two towers are joined by a long gabled hall, notable for its large Gothic windows. The hall was originally aisled by timber posts and was accessible from the

The Tudor gatehouse at Stokesay

upper floor of the north tower. The timbered roof is a fine example of medieval craftsmanship, supported by three pairs of crucks, the upper parts of which are still in position, supported on stone pilasters which were built to replace the rotted lower parts of the timbers. At the south end of the hall, a solar was built, with access only by an outer staircase, covered in at some point. The solar had two 'squints' through which the occupants could see what was going on in the hall, which had an octagonal central hearth made of stone, but later rooms were well equipped with wall fireplaces.

A so-called 'passage block' led from the solar to a small room between it and the south tower, but there was no access to this tower except from the courtyard. The tower walls are over five feet thick and have corbelled garderobes built into them which discharged into the moat. The kitchen block stood beside the north tower. Its foundations can still be traced on the ground, though it disappeared long ago. The well near the south tower is fifty feet deep.

In the sixteenth century, by which time Laurence de Ludlow's descendants had married into the Vernon family of Haddon Hall, Derbyshire, an exuberant half-timbered gatehouse, somewhat incongruous but irresistibly picturesque, was built across the courtyard. There are some interesting carvings on the oak timbers, including Adam and Eve and the serpent. The fine timber panelling and the Flemish overmantel of carved oak now to be seen in the solar were added by the seventeenth-century occupiers, the Baldwyn family who leased the place for six generations from the descendants of Dame Elizabeth Craven, who had acquired the 'castle' in 1620. It had clearly never been intended to stand up to any kind of serious attack, and in fact it came under threat more from the English than from the Welsh, when Cromwell's troops laid siege to it in 1645. The Royalist occupants gave up without a fight, and it is a nice irony that for the unique survival of so much of this fine medieval manor house we are indebted to their cowardice in the face of the enemy, for their hasty surrender meant that the building suffered only minimal damage. The curtain wall was demolished except for a small section which remains near the south tower. It originally stood thirty-four feet above the moat and was several feet thick, with battlemented parapets.

The Baldwyns sub-let the property to the local farmers who brought it to ruin faster than all the Welsh marauders and Puritan troops together. In 1869, however, Stokesay was sold to the Allcroft family, who have owned it since and have taken great care to restore and preserve this fine medieval building for all to see and enjoy.

Only a few miles away from Stokesay, and built very soon afterwards, is the so-called Acton Burnell Castle. It is a ruin now – no more than a red sandstone shell – but it was built by Robert Burnell, Bishop of Bath and Wells and Edward I's Lord Chancellor. He was granted his licence to crenellate in 1284. The house is in the form of a tower house, with four projecting and battlemented towers at the corners, and looks formidable enough, but it had no moat and its entrances were at ground-floor level, on ground which had no natural defensive lie. The hall was on the upper floor with the solar, and one tower contained the chapel while another had garderobes with drainage channels. It has been suggested on grounds of style of windows in the building that it must have remained unfinished when the Bishop died in 1292.

In the field beside the ruins are two large stone gables, which are thought to be the end walls of what would have been the four were executed in the conflict which was no longer between English and Welsh but between Yorkists and Lancastrians. The place is also associated in folklore with Jack o' Kent, a medieval magician who had sold his soul to the devil when he was only a boy. He had flying horses, which he is said to have kept in the cellars of Kentchurch Court.

Hampton Court (in the same county) was built a little later than Kentchurch, Sir Rowland Lenthall obtaining his licence to crenellate in 1434. This house also has been drastically remodelled, but several parts of the medieval fortified house remain, including the battlemented gatehouse, the porch to the great hall, standing across a courtyard, and the chapel, with its fine ribbed ceiling and some original stained glass. From the road the place looks almost like a toy castle at the end of the drive.

In the other Welsh border county, Cheshire, Brimstead Hall and Doddington Castle are roughly contemporary. Sir Hugh de Hulse was lord of the manor at Brimstage, and a licence to build an oratory was granted him in 1398, in the tower house which had three storeys, with a turret at one corner in which there were garderobes and a spiral staircase. The chapel may have been the vaulted ground-floor room, with small square windows. The top floor with its battlements and flat stone roof later went through some change, and the extended house became a farmhouse.

Doddington Castle was also a fortified house, licence to crenellate having been granted to Sir John Delves by Edward III. The house was built of the local red sandstone, in the style of the northern pele towers, with a tunnel-vaulted room on the ground floor. The 'castle' was occupied by Cromwell's troops during the Civil War, and subsequently a new house was built on higher ground in a park landscaped by 'Capability' Brown, this building eventually becoming a school with the old fortified manor house remaining in its grounds.

Little Wenham Hall in Suffolk was built at a similar date to Stokesay and was a fortified house from the start, built of very early brick, with flint and stone dressings and wall bases. It was probably begun when Sir John de Vaux was lord of the manor, but not completed until after Petronella of Nerford had acquired the manor in 1287, for represented on a boss in the chapel is her namesake Saint Petronella, who suffered martyrdom under the Romans. The building represents an intermediate stage between the castle and the manor house principle. You could hardly find a more peaceful spot to induce a feeling of security than this

Ruins of Acton Burnell Castle, Shropshire, showing the end gable of a former barn through the doorway

Bishop's very large barn, for they are 150 feet apart. When Edward I was preoccupied with military matters in the west, he held a Parliament at Acton Burnell, the village giving its name to a statute which marked the growing importance of trade by providing for the prompt recovery of debts. It is believed that this Parliament met in the great barn, and if so, it would indicate that the Bishop's house was habitable before he was given licence to crenellate, for he must have entertained the King there, and the statute's date is 1283.

In Herefordshire, Kentchurch Court, although substantially an eighteenth-century rebuilding by Nash and now standing peacefully in its own deer park, started life as the manor house of the Scudamore family, well fortified against the Welsh threat, and a tower and gateway remain from the medieval building. The tower had its staircase in the thick walls, and there was a garderobe projecting on one side of this house beside a tributary of the River Monmow, very near the Welsh border. The tower is usually attributed to Owain Glyndwr, one of whose daughters, Alice, married Sir John Scudamore, only to lose her husband and her three sons after the Battle of Mortimer's Cross, when all

Little Wenham Hall, Suffolk

secluded place in what we now call the Constable country, but caution was well advised in those days, and the hall was built above a brick-vaulted basement and reached by an outer stone staircase. The house was only partly enclosed by a moat, however.

The chapel at Little Wenham adjoins the hall in an L shape with the usual clockwise newel staircase in the re-entrant angle between them. The solar was over the chapel in this case. In the hall, a laver with a traceried stone arch is in the wall, with a drain at the back and an iron hook hanging from the top, which perhaps supported a lead pipe coming down from a tank above. A demolished extension to the hall may have been a garderobe. The doorway to the chapel, which has a piscina, is flanked by small windows with wooden shutters. Clearly, the lord of the manor here was thinking as much about comfortable living as about defence.

Godlingstone Manor, near Swanage in Dorset, was a semi-fortified house, built of stone around 1300. It has an unusual semi-circular tower at one end, not high but substantial. It is a

Haddon Hall, Derbyshire, from the south

farmhouse now but was once owned by families with illustrious names such as Talbot and Pole.

Haddon Hall itself, though semi-fortified, was never anything remotely like a castle, and although this mellow and delightfully romantic stone house on the bank of the River Wye became a palace of the earls and dukes of Rutland, it began its life as the manor house of the Peverel family, whose first lord was an illegitimate son of William the Conqueror. They sub-let it to the Avenells, through whom it passed in about 1170 to Richard de Vernon, and he it was who first obtained permission to fortify the house in 1195, although the crenellation of the present building is later than that. Some masonry of the twelfth century remains, however, particularly in Peverel's Tower and the walls adjacent to it, and in the walls of the chapel. The chapel contains fine fifteenth-century wall paintings and stained glass windows.

The nucleus of the Vernon manor house was built around 1370 by the fourth Sir Richard Vernon and included great hall, parlour, kitchen and other service rooms, in a wing across the former large courtyard, dividing it into two smaller ones. The outside interest of the house includes gargoyles and a stone dovecote. Much alteration and addition was done here in the Elizabethan and Jacobean periods, but the medieval survivals are most interesting. They include stone troughs for the storage of water in the kitchen, a painted ceiling in the solar, an outer staircase to the chapel, and in the hall, a fine panelled screen with minstrels' gallery above. At the other end of the hall, the dais for the high table is lit by a traceried window.

The romantic tradition of Haddon is, of course, the famous tale of Dorothy Vernon's supposed elopement in 1567 with Sir John Manners, through whom the manor house became a ducal palace, and as we owe the preservation of Stokesay to cowardice, we owe the preservation of Haddon to neglect, for when the Manners moved their chief seat to Belvoir Castle and left Haddon Hall for more than two hundred years to the bats and owls, as one old writer put it, they at least unwittingly preserved it from the appalling attentions of Georgian and Victorian 'improvers'.

We have noticed, in this and previous chapters, several ostensibly fortified houses which could not have stood up to any serious hostilities, but we must also take account of some which were put up with all seriousness against real dangers. Sir Edward Dalyngrigge was given a licence to fortify his manor house at Bodiam in Sussex in 1386, against French attack, but instead he pulled it down and built the strong moated castle we see there now – needlessly, as it happened. The citadel scarcely had a shot fired at it.

Cooling Castle was a manor house fortified under licence to Sir John de Cobham between 1381 and 1385, in the same period of alarm about possible invasion by the French, and he attached a plate to the gatehouse to make it clear to everyone that his object was not personal safety but patriotism, as part of the improved defences needed to protect London's vulnerable position from the Thames:

> Knouwyth that beeth and schal be
> That I am mad in help of the cuntre
> In knowying of whyche thyng
> Thys is chartre and wytnessyng.

The 'castle' was hardly sited with great strategic flair, however, being three miles from the river on the low and level marshland of north Kent, but it was moated and had a strong-looking battlemented gatehouse with twin towers. Any other defences it may once have had have since vanished in the modernization of the house, except for sections of its curtain wall.

The place was defended for a period early in the fifteenth century against the messengers of the Archbishop of Canterbury rather than the armies of France, when it was occupied by the Lollard rebel Sir John Oldcastle, who acquired it through his marriage with Joan de la Pole and became Baron Cobham before he became notorious. He presented the living of the parish in his gift to a priest who spoke heresy from the pulpit, and he corresponded from Cooling with Hussite leaders in Europe. Eventually he shut the gates against an officer bringing him a summons from the Primate but soon found himself in the Tower and subject to excommunication. Escaping from his prison, he spent three years travelling secretly about the country with a price on his head and organized an abortive rising before being caught and conveyed again to London, where he was hanged and burnt. Oldcastle was certainly the leading, but not the only landlord of the period who identified himself with the teachings of Wycliffe against ecclesiastical corruption.

Some surviving fortified manor houses, like Haddon Hall and Broughton Castle, are in what would seem like the comparative safety of the Midlands. They were built at a time when the transition from castles to manor houses, and then to undefended houses, was taking place in most parts of England, and there can be little doubt that in many cases these miniature 'castles' were built purely as status symbols – flamboyant expressions of the wealth and power of the high officials or retired military men who lived in them, and they had no real defensive function unless against burglars or rebellious peasants. Nevertheless, fortifications was a practice which was to continue into the early sixteenth century, its most concentrated occurrence being, however, in the north of England during the fourteenth century, when Edward I's failure to bring Scotland under control of the English Crown led to a long period of almost continuous inter-baronial warfare and border raiding.

Thirty years after Stokesay, the new king granted a licence to the Markenfield family in Yorkshire. In an isolated spot near Ripon John de Markenfield erected his L-shaped manor house in grey stone with a moat round it and the minimum of defensive walls, although the hall was built on the upper floor, just in case. Ground-floor halls were becoming much more common in other parts of England by this time. Like Stokesay, it has a Tudor

A vaulted room in Markenfield Hall, North Yorkshire

gatehouse at the entrance to its courtyard – since used as a farmyard – reached by a stone bridge across the moat. The hall is above the kitchen and cellar and as usual was accessible by an outside stone stairway. As well as the hall, there was a chapel on the first floor, with an ambry, a piscina and the family arms. The Markenfields' Catholic sympathies, however, led to their forfeiture of the manor when they supported Mary Stuart's claim to the throne in 1569, and Elizabeth gave the property to her Lord Chancellor, Baron Ellesmere. Victorian farm buildings keep the empty manor house company now at the end of a long lane. It is a little-known place, yet within a stone's throw of Fountains Abbey, which was a crowded, busy and magnificent Cistercian establishment when Markenfield Hall was built.

The manor of Spofforth, in West Yorkshire, was one of the eighty-six granted by the Conqueror to William de Percy, founder of that great northern family which later became more closely associated with Northumberland. Henry de Percy was licensed to crenellate his manor house at Spofforth in 1308, though it does not seem to have been given the heavy fortifications one might

Spofforth Castle, West Yorkshire

expect. It had a great hall above an aisled undercroft, and a solar above the kitchen, which had two fireplaces. The stair turret was capped with a sort of short spire. Sir Henry Percy, the famous Hotspur, was born in this house, before it was brought to ruin for the first but by no means the only time. Its final demolition took place in the Civil War.

Aydon Castle in Northumberland was another of the early fortifications. A licence was granted in 1305 to the owner of this house between the River Tyne and the Roman wall, and the hall range – built around 1280 – was surrounded by square walls to form a bailey, which became an inner bailey when further defensive walls were added to the north. The hall of the original house had already been put with circumspection on the first floor, with an outside stone staircase, parallel to the wall, leading into a screens passage. The room below it had a large fireplace, though the hall itself had none, and this lower room may have been used by the lord's men-at-arms as well as being the kitchen until a new one was built fifty years later. A solar wing was at the high table end of the hall, and this had a fireplace, too. A hollow buttress at one corner contained a garderobe and drainage pit. The 'castle' was situated in a well-defended natural position, and it was not felt necessary to build a tower or keep.

Generally, however, the keep or tower house was the type of defensive building favoured in the far north long after it had disappeared elsewhere. Such buildings are usually called pele towers, and they were occupied by other men of property, such as village parsons, as well as those lords whose status did not run to castles. They were generally three-storey buildings, the ground floor having no windows but only narrow slits for ventilation. The owner's livestock might be kept there in times of danger, for the red-haired Caledonian barbarians not only burnt churches and killed women and children but stole cattle and other property as well. The hall was on the first floor of the tower, and a bower, or private room similar to the solar in less defensive houses, was on the second floor.

It is not always possible to equate fortified houses in the north with the feudal manors of the country farther south, but Burneside Hall and Preston Patrick, one north and one south of Kendal, in Cumbria, were both fourteenth-century tower houses with domestic extensions of later date. Preston Patrick is the more impressive of the two, with a central hall range between cross wings. The hall is quite small. There are tunnel-vaulted rooms and passages in both houses, and Preston Patrick has a straight interior staircase alongside a wall between the hall and service rooms, leading to what is called the Court Room.

Farther north, near Penrith, is Dacre Castle, a battlemented tower house which is very nearly a castle in the military sense, with turrets at each corner of a solid square keep. In fact, it was built early in the fourteenth century on the site of an older castle there. The Dacre family entered their house at ground level, though, in the west tower where a spiral staircase led to the upper rooms. They were granted licence for a private chapel in 1354. In the hall there is an unusually decorative domestic laver in one wall, with an arched top and floral-shaped bowl with twelve petals. The later Dacres supported Mary Tudor and were sacked by Elizabeth's cousin, Lord Hunsdon.

Sizergh Castle is one of the most outstanding examples of the pele tower type. The lord of the manor here as the head of the Strickland family, who were at Sizergh from 1239 onwards. Walter Strickland raised an army of a thousand men in 1297 to take part in Edward I's invasion of Scotland, and in return he was made a Knight of the Bath and granted Free Warren on his land. The large square tower dates from about 1340, and it seems that the former house was demolished to make way for this at a time when Edward III was resuming hostilities against the Scots. The tower's dimensions are sixty by forty feet, with a height of sixty feet, and the walls are ten feet thick at the base, where there is a tunnel-vaulted basement.

In the mid-fifteenth century, when the Scottish threat was less menacing, the Stricklands built a hall range next to the pele tower, but a great deal of alteration went on here in the Eliza-bethan period, when further wings were added, and in the eighteenth century, so that little of the medieval house is now visible. Sizergh is, in fact, famous for its high-quality Eliza-bethan woodwork, chimney-pieces and ceilings, and on the top floor of the pele tower a small museum displays relics of Bonnie Prince Charlie, turning the long fear of the north to modern advantage.

Yanwath Hall near Penrith is a little older than Sizergh. The pele tower here was built early in the fourteenth century by John de Sutton. The ground floor is tunnel-vaulted, and the first floor has the royal arms over the fireplace. In the following century a hall and kitchen range were built on to it, the hall having a bay window at its high table end. The hall was divided to form two floors later, and eventually this house, which is now a rather splendid farmhouse, came into the possession of those Cumbrian empire-builders the Lowther family.

A pele tower relegated to a barn stands at Beetham, dating from the mid-fourteenth century, and this too was extended later to form a fortified manor house with great hall, solar and private chapel. A turret staircase was placed between the hall and solar.

At Greystoke, William de Greystoke was granted a licence to fortify his house in 1353, and his massive pele tower remains behind a more recent house built by Salvin for the Duke of Norfolk. The barony of Greystoke had been created around 1120 by Henry I, not – unusually – for one of the French aristocracy but for a descendant of an English family which had held the extensive manor since before the Conquest. A ghost story is associated with this tower, the apparition being a guest of the Duke's who disappeared there during the night after a day's hunting in the deer park.

Hutton-in-the-Forest is a largely modern house, with an assortment of dates and styles, but it began as a medieval manor house when Thomas de Hoton built a pele tower in the mid-fourteenth century. This had a spiral staircase in one corner. The wealthy merchant family of Fletcher bought the property in the early seventeenth century and made much alteration to it.

Kentmere Hall, further south, may have had its pele tower built merely to follow the fashion of the north, although Scots cattle-raiders may have threatened from time to time. It is a ruin now, but it was built in the fourteenth century by the de Gilpin family. It was tunnel-vaulted on the ground floor and had the usual corner staircase. The existing farmhouse was built on in the following century, and legend has it that a thirty-foot oak beam inside was lifted into position by Hugh Heard, the Troutbeck giant, after ten men had tried to raise it without success. Bernard de Gilpin was born in this house in 1517. He became Archdeacon of Durham and was known as the Apostle of the North for his good works throughout the wild country of northern England.

Workington Hall, on the coast, is also a ruin. Sir Gilbert de Curwen fortified his house in 1379, under licence from Richard II. In the following century, the pele tower was incorporated in a larger house with a great hall, and in the seventeenth century the house with its deer park was described as one of the fairest in the land. Sir Henry Curwen had received Mary, Queen of Scots, here on her way to Carlisle.

Back in Northumberland, meanwhile, Featherstone Castle had been fortified around 1330 by the addition of a tower to one end of an existing hall-house near the South Tyne river. This was followed by many others over a long period of time, including Langley Castle and Haughton Castle, both of the tower-house type, the latter on the north side of Hadrian's Wall. Haughton village survived the Caledonian threat only to succumb to the designs of a nineteenth-century landlord who destroyed the village to create his park.

Bywell, near the southern border of Northumberland, was a prosperous iron town in the Middle Ages, with two churches, for the two baronies of Baliol and Bolbec had their common manorial boundary there after the Conquest. Its fortified tower house was built in the fifteenth century using Roman materials. It had a vaulted ground-floor room with two chambers on the floor above it, and a single room above that with a garderobe in the corner.

The pele tower, as such, did not extend as far south as Yorkshire, but Nappa Hall, near Askrigg, is a fortified manor

Nappa Hall, North Yorkshire

house of about 1460 with a hall joining two towers of unequal height. The Metcalfe family built here a solid tower of four storeys with battlements at the west end, whilst the smaller east tower housed the kitchen and other service rooms.

Mortham Tower, farther north, was probably built a little earlier. It consisted of a tower house in a courtyard with a battlemented curtain wall round it, though it was much altered at a later date by the Rokeby family. It had been built on the site of an earlier tower house destroyed by the Scots after the Battle of Bannockburn, together with the whole village and its chapel. Some of the church's gravestones were built into the masonry of the fortified manor's new gateway when the house was rebuilt some years afterwards.

Whilst all this fortification against the Scots was going on in the north, lords of more southerly manors were applying to the king for licences to secure themselves against other threats, even if, in some cases, the only danger was being out of fashion.

Greys Court in Oxfordshire probably falls into the latter category, since there could have been little to defend against in

The ruins of Greys Court, Oxfordshire

the Thames valley below the Chilterns in 1347, when Sir John de Grey was granted a licence to crenellate. The de Greys had been here since the Conquest, but it is said that one Lord Grey nearly lost his estate through drawing a knife in anger in the presence of the King. At any rate, the fortified house consisted of a rectangular walled courtyard or bailey with a tower at each corner and a square tower of four storeys in the enclosure, built of flint and brick. This house is in ruins now. A daughter of Lord Grey of Rotherfield, Maud, was married to Sir Thomas Harcourt of Stanton Harcourt in 1394, and a stone effigy in the village church there is thought to be hers.

The Knollys family acquired this manor in 1518 and they built the new house, also of brick and flint, with a well-house in the courtyard, where water was drawn by means of a large donkey-wheel which can still be seen. It was in this house that the Earl and Countess of Somerset were detained in the custody of Lord Knollys when they were convicted of the murder of Sir Thomas Overbury.

Broughton Castle, at the northern end of the same county,

was originally a manor house owned by Sir John de Broughton, who built it around 1300. It may have been given its wide moat at that time. There is an effigy of a knight in the village church which may well be Sir John, who died in 1315. His son was granted licence to worship in the private chapel in 1331. But William of Wykeham bought the manor subsequently, and it was his great-nephew, Sir Thomas Wykeham, who sought, and was granted, licence to crenellate in 1405. The 'castle' then passed by marriage to the Fiennes family, whose heads became the Lords Say and Sele, and it has been their property ever since. Some alteration was done in the sixteenth century, but the medieval house is still apparent.

It consisted of the customary great hall, which was quite large for the time – fifty-four by nearly thirty feet, similar to that at Stokesay Castle. The kitchen and offices were at one end of the solar and chapel at the other, on the first floor with a vaulted undercroft beneath. The building has a vaulted passage and a projecting garderobe tower. The chapel is perhaps the most interesting room at Broughton, however, being one of the finest medieval domestic chapels remaining. It is of two-storey height, with an original stone altar and piscina, and it has a priest's room from which a squint looks into the chapel, whilst another permits a view of the chapel from the solar.

A large part of the manor – nearly three-quarters of the parish – was enclosed here as early as the reign of Elizabeth I, when Sir Richard Fiennes turned it into private pasture land. The first Viscount Saye and Sele, who was nicknamed 'Old Subtility', was among the leading organizers of Puritan opposition to Charles I, and it is said that Hampden, Pym and others met here and that soldiers for Cromwell's army were drilled and lodged here. The castle was not fortified well enough to resist Royalist troops, however, and surrendered under attacks which left bullet marks on the curtain wall to the west.

Woodsford Castle, near the coast in Dorset, has been known also as Woodsford-Strangways, having been owned by the Strangways family who restored it after it had fallen into ruin, but it declined to farmhouse status all the same and was given, of all things, a thatched roof! Nevertheless, its defensive intent is obvious enough. It was built of Purbeck limestone by Sir William de Whitfield, who was granted his licence to crenellate in 1335, but by 1368 the property had come into the ownership of Sir Guy de Bryan, whose family name recurs in Dorset place-names such as Hazelbury Bryan and Bryanston School. The manor house had five projecting towers round its two-storey central range, in which the great hall, chapel and private rooms were above tunnel-vaulted service rooms below. One tower had garderobes while the chapel had a piscina and the solar a laver.

In Somerset, Sir John de la Mare was given his licence in 1373, to fortify his mansion at Nunney, and he turned it into a fairly well defended place within a moat which was itself partly enclosed by a curtain wall, but comforts were certainly in the mind of Sir John, who was a veteran of the French wars, and his 'castle' may have had more to do with status than with fear of attack. It was certainly not built in a good strategic position, for it stands in the village street across the road from the church, and its entrance was on the ground floor. The great hall was upstairs, reached by a straight staircase, and the solar and chapel were higher still in this narrow oblong building with conically capped towers at each corner. Part of this ruin collapsed as recently as 1910, having stood, weakened by siege and partially demolished, since the Civil War.

Combe Sydenham Hall, near Williton, is an Elizabethan house in general, but it incorporates the remains of a medieval house and has a tower which was originally one of several, so I suppose the place could be called a semi-fortified manor house, though it stands beside the road in a hollow and could scarcely have been defended. Indeed it suffered at the hands of Cromwell's men in the Civil War. It was first built in 1360, but it was George Sydenham who rebuilt it in 1580, sub-dividing the great hall to form a room above it and putting a staircase in the one lofty grey tower which he retained, though a newel staircase remains as well as a huge wall fireplace.

An odd legend here was connected with a meteorite kept in the entrance hall and thought by some to be a cannon-ball. George Sydenham's daughter was that Elizabeth whom Sir Francis Drake married in 1585, two years after his first wife died. It is said that after his betrothal to Miss Sydenham, he left on one of his voyages, telling her that however long he might be away, he would send her a token of his well-being. Elizabeth, however, lost patience after a time and became engaged to someone else, but when the couple were about to get married, the meteorite rolled between them of its own accord, and the girl changed her mind and awaited the return of Sir Francis.

Amberley Castle in Sussex dates – as an unquestionably real castle – from 1377, when Bishop Rede of Chichester obtained a licence to crenellate in the year when the French burnt Rye.

Unlike Bodiam, however, which replaced the former buildings on the site, Amberley incorporated the existing manor house within its structure. This probably dates from the early thirteenth century. A curtain wall and gatehouse were built round a new great hall, to which the older small manor house became an appendage. Its hall was converted into a chapel by taking out its floor and turning it into a ground-floor room near the new hall. The buildings also included a lodging house for the bishop's mercenaries. The castle was sacked during the Civil War, and much alteration took place there afterwards, so that the present ruins show little of the original house.

Hever Castle in Kent, if not actually a ruin when William Waldorf Astor rescued it from oblivion in 1903, was at any rate no more than a humble farmhouse, so that it is hardly surprising that its character has been changed rather drastically in the present century. But it was built as a manor house by William de Hever and passed by marriage into the Cobham family. It was Sir John de Cobham who was granted licence to fortify the place by Richard II. The house was surrounded by a rectangular moat, and although little of its genuine medieval character remains, it is clear that comforts were as important as defence in the mind of its builder. When the Bullens became lords of the manor late in the fifteenth century, they carried out some alterations, and it was soon good enough to accommodate the King, even if His Majesty's flamboyant expectations could perhaps be subdued in the interests of his passion for Sir Thomas Bullen's black-eyed daughter. But Henry took over the place and used it as a prison after his change of heart, and it never recovered its former status.

In Essex, Faulkbourne Hall was originally a timber-framed manor house, but when Sir John Montgomery was given his licence to crenellate in 1439, during the disordered period of Henry VI's reign, he carried out his building programme in brick, which was by then coming into widespread use for country houses, especially in the eastern counties where there was no stone, and for churches as well, particularly here in Essex. This manor became the property of the Bullock family, and there are several good monuments to them in the Norman village church.

Baconsthorpe Castle, in Norfolk, was built over a period of thirty-five years from about 1450 – a somewhat excessive time for a building intended for defence, one might think. Sir Henry Heydon was the author of this fortified house enclosed, with its home farm, by a moat and reached by a three-storey gatehouse with a vaulted passage. The building is faced with knapped flint. The manor house ruins stand near an eighteenth-century mansion which gave new employment to much of the 'castle's' redundant stone.

Mannington Hall, near Saxthorpe, Norfolk, was built after 1451, when a licence was granted by Henry VI, and the fortified house was erected in brick and flint and surrounded by a moat but does not seem to have been heavily fortified. It is said that Oliver Cromwell stayed here several times with the Potts family who owned it then. The extensive alterations carried out by the Earl of Orford in the nineteenth century make it difficult to tell what the medieval house looked like. It is still in the possession of the Walpole family. The Prime Minister's descendant who came into the title in 1846 was a misogynist, and the house is known more for its defences against women than against any medieval intruders, having several pathetic inscriptions on the walls, one of which says: 'There is no good woman, and if one attains to any good I know not how an ill-made thing becomes good.'

Sir Edmund Bedingfield, lord of the manor of Oxburgh, not far away, apparently fortified his house against marauding bands of unemployed mercenaries in 1482. He would have had no opposition from the new king, Richard III, for he was one of Richard's favourites. He built a large house with a courtyard and surrounded it with a wide square moat, across the drawbridge of which one entered via a huge gatehouse. This, alas, is the only part surviving from the medieval house, as Sir Richard Bedingfield pulled down the hall range in the eighteenth century. But the gatehouse is interesting enough, rising eighty feet above the water into a castellated tower of brick, with gun-loops and arrow-slits. What is more, the arch above the top window over the drawbridge was provided with holes from which boiling oil and other deterrents could be poured on anyone with the gall to attack the place. The builder must have been an extremely insecure fellow.

One of his descendants, Sir Henry, became Bloody Mary's Constable of the Tower, despite being a bumbling Norfolk squire with whom Elizabeth became much exasperated when he had her in his charge at Woodstock, for he did everything by the book and had no imagination. When Elizabeth came to the throne, she dismissed Bedingfield at once and sent him home to Norfolk, saying: 'If we have any prisoner whom we would have

sharply and straitly kept, then we will send for you.' Still, she visited him at Oxburgh twenty years later. It was part of the political strategy of the Tudor monarchs to make progresses through the houses of their more powerful subjects, taking huge retinues with them, expecting lavish hospitality and thus draining their hosts' financial resources and keeping their ambitions in check. At Oxburgh, the Bedingfields survived this assault, and the family lives there still.

Nothing but a few fragments remains above ground of Gresham Castle, a fortified manor house licensed in 1319, but we know a little about it because it came into the possession of the Pastons, whose letters are such valuable sources of social history in the fifteenth century. It was a quadrangular building with a moat round it, and Margaret Paston feared for its safety when she wrote to her husband John, who was in London, with a shopping list which included pole-axes and crossbows as well as cloth and groceries. But these precautions were of no avail, for the place was sacked by Lord Moleyns in 1448, and John Paston petitioned the King, describing how a thousand men 'arrayed in manner of war' had turned up with weapons and equipment, including 'picks with which they mined down the walls, and long trees with which they broke up gates and doors', and had driven out his wife and others who were in the house before wrecking the rest of it and stealing its contents – 'stuff, array and money to the value of £200'. The Roses wars were uneasy times for many in rural England who suffered at the hands of lawless gentry who might be committing piracy one day and sitting on the King's Bench the next. But it was only a temporary setback for the Pastons. They were on their way up from modest peasant origins, as we shall see later.

Compton Castle in Devon, not far from Torquay, must be one of the last manor houses to be fortified for genuine defensive reasons, when the Gilberts built a massive stone shield round their fourteenth-century house, in about 1530, against French raiders. In doing so, they converted it into an impressive fortress, which is still lived in by the Gilberts, but alas, not a great deal of the original manor remains, the present great hall being a modern reconstruction. The tunnel-vaulted chapel dates from 1420.

Sir John Gilbert was responsible for the fortification. He and his brothers Humphrey and Adrian were the sons of Otho Gilbert and his wife, who later married again, bearing her second husband the child who became Sir Walter Raleigh and

Oxburgh Hall, Norfolk, from the north-west

who is shown with his half-brother Humphrey Gilbert in Millais' famous painting *The Boyhood of Raleigh*. Humphrey was the discoverer of Newfoundland. The fifteenth-century rebuilding of Compton provided the former smallish manor house with two courtyards, ample garderobes and formidable defences, but one of its most interesting features today is the sixteenth-century kitchen with its vast fireplace and a more ordinary domestic detail which perhaps enables us to feel closer to the people of the house than all the formal history and architecture we can read. It is just a hollow in the stone by the door, made by centuries of sharpening the cooks' knives in the traditional spot.

Compton Castle, Devon

Little Moreton Hall, Cheshire

CHAPTER 4

The Home Made Island

By the end of the fourteenth century, apart from those vulnerable areas we have been looking at in the previous chapter, kitchen knives were being sharpened instead of swords and daggers in most of the manor houses of England, and English was being spoken instead of French. Castle building had ceased, and the lords were building themselves manor houses in which they looked for the architecture of comfortable living instead of the architecture of military expediency. They built their homes, as they had previously built their castles, according to their wealth and position in the land, but their positions as lords of manors were different from what they had been a century or more earlier. The feudal system was on its last legs.

The lord or his bailiff now tended to hire men for wages, experience having shown that the lord's land was better cultivated by paid men working throughout the year than by peasants who grudgingly left their own strips on certain days to attend to their lord's land. There was also a change in the concept of agriculture as a means of self-sufficiency. Instead of producing food just for their own consumption, there was a demand for produce to be supplied to the markets of growing urban populations. The serfs saved money from their earnings and purchased their freedom, and as the lords often could not pay enough to keep their demesnes cultivated, they began to let their land on lease to a new class of worker, the yeoman or tenant farmer.

Serfdom continued, but it was on its way out, if only slowly. Some argue that the Peasants' Revolt delayed the abolition of serfdom, and indeed, complete emancipation was not achieved until the late Tudor period, when Elizabeth made it compulsory for all remaining serfs or villeins to purchase their freedom – at a crippling price, naturally. But the nails were being hammered in the coffin lid of feudal slavery before Richard III died at Bosworth.

The knights and their squires, performing military service in return for land, had gone, too, and the crusading impulse was dying out. Armies were raised by paying men to be soldiers, and romantic tales of heroic knights in their coats of mail, and young swains courting superior ladies, began to fade from the troubadours' repertoire, sadly perhaps, for the age of chivalry undoubtedly raised the status of women, if only a little. The male-dominated society of earlier times, in which women were rarely mentioned in the literature, was being slowly broken down. Not that the old spirit of male chauvinism had died altogether. At Dawlish, Devon, in 1301, the manorial court was told that a farmer's wife, Agnes Day, would not have anything to do with her husband because Matthew, the squire (who had gone to Rome), had a child by her, and she scorned her husband. The best the court could say to this was that if Matthew should return from Rome, 'they do not think that he will frequent her.' The new heroes of the time were outlaws like Robin Hood, who bucked the system.

As for the lords themselves, they had increased their share in the government of the realm since Magna Carta, but their domestic powers were less tyrannous than they had been, except in the Welsh and northern marches where the barons were a law unto themselves. They were still powerful, of course, and although in theory all men may have been more or less equal in the eyes of the law, some were in practice more equal than others. A wealthy lord could manipulate both judge and jury, and he still punished petty crimes in the manorial court with fines which went into his pocket. But agricultural workers now had some bargaining power and saw themselves as tenants by manorial custom, with a legal claim on the land they held. The depressed economy forced the lords to some extent to recognize what they would formerly have suppressed rigorously as being against their own private interests, and by a judgement of 1467 it became law that no lord had a right to oust a customary tenant, who 'is as well inheritor to have the land to him and his heirs according to the custom of the manor as any man is to have his lands at common law'. Ordinary people were now able to change their employers or landlords when they pleased, for more money or better land, so that the lords could no longer afford to ride roughshod over their tenants and employees.

They might build fine houses and enjoy the expensive sport of the hunt (which they had wrested from the king's monopoly and made the almost exclusive activity of 'gentlemen', punishing severely any ordinary folk caught poaching). But the social order was less stable than it had been, and life for the lords was more competitive, since their wealth could now slip backwards through mismanagement of their affairs. The civil Wars of the Roses, largely the creation of the Marcher lords who had not relaxed their feudal grip, marked the end of the great feudal barons, for it gave the Tudors the opportunity to trim the beards of over-powerful subjects, and they were succeeded by a larger class of landowners with smaller fortunes and less power.

In the meantime, however, the lords had to keep up appearances to try to maintain their positions, and fifteenth-century manor houses reflect the general optimism of their builders before the inevitable happened. The house surrounded by a moat, once a necessary instrument of defence, now became merely fashionable. The home-made island with its ring of bright water not only added a touch of the picturesque to the lord's dwelling but also set it apart from the vulgar homes of the peasantry. No man is an island, perhaps, but a manor house might be. It is not surprising that surviving fifteenth-century manor houses are among the most popular of historic buildings with tourists today, for they combine their picturesque qualities with that image sacred to the Englishman, spelled out by the Elizabethan lawyer Sir Edward Coke, that his home is his castle, 'as well for his defence against injury and violence as for his repose'.

The type was characterized in the late fourteenth century by the small manor house at Lower Brockhampton, near Bromyard in Herefordshire. The place is very pretty – not only the house itself but the whole setting, which is in peaceful farming country rich with orchards. The house is situated in a wooded valley and almost surrounded by its moat, which a fit man could probably jump without getting his feet wet, so it was never conceived as having a defensive function, and there is no doubt that the lord of the manor who lived here was what we would nowadays call a gentleman farmer. Ducks paddle happily on the moat today, and herons pay it visits. The house is reached via a small timber-framed gatehouse with one jettied room above the passage through it. This was built in the fifteenth century but is completely in character with the house and adds much to its charm. Part of the original house has disappeared, but the surviving central range and one wing include the hall with a spere truss which held the screen. The ruins of a Norman chapel stand nearby.

A more ambitious manor house of the type was built at

Manor and gatehouse, Lower Brockhampton, Hereford & Worcester

Groombridge, Kent, very early in the last century of medieval England. The setting here is magnificent, too, though rather different from Herefordshire, but the house there now is a Palladian-style building of brick and stone attributed to Wren. The wide moat, however, survives from the fifteenth century, when the lord of the manor was Sir Richard Waller, who brought Charles, Duke of Orleans, prisoner here after Agincourt and kept him for twenty-five years before releasing him for a ransome of 400,000 crowns.

Thomas Chaucer, son of the poet, also fought at Agincourt, and after his death his daughter Alice inherited the manor of Ewelme in the Oxfordshire Chilterns. Her first husband was Thomas de Montacute, Earl of Salisbury, who owned, among other places, that ancient manor we noticed at Luddesdown in Kent and who died in France just before Joan of Arc rallied the native troops against the English. Before Joan was brought to the stake, Alice was married again, this time to William de la Pole, who had also been in France and was soon made Duke of Suffolk. At Ewelme, the Duke and Duchess began the building

Groombridge Place, Kent, from the north-west

of a model village with a school and a hospital for thirteen poor men, as well as their palace. They rebuilt the village church about the same time, in the 1430s.

The old moated manor house of the Chaucer family was enlarged into a palace, mainly by Alice after her second husband's ignominious end in a boat off Dover when he was trying to escape to France. The manor house and the other secular buildings were among the earliest brick buildings in Oxfordshire, and the Duke is thought to have brought builders from his estates at Wingfield in East Anglia, where brick was in very early use. The redoubtable Margaret of Anjou, Henry VI's widow, lived here with Duchess Alice for a time in lenient imprisonment, and later Henry VIII and Elizabeth both used the house, Henry having spent his honeymoon here with Catherine Howard.

Leland described the place in 1542 as 'set within a fair moat and builded richly of brick and stone. The hall of it is fair and hath great bars of iron over thwart it instead of cross beams.' It had a two-storey range of dwellings for the servants. By early in the following century, however, the house was in ruins, and it has now entirely disappeared except for one or two fragments in the Georgian manor house on the site.

Thomas Chaucer held some land at Gresham in Norfolk early in the fifteenth century, and this manor is also associated with the Pastons, whom we might pause to consider at this point, for their family correspondence is so valuable a source of information about the minor nobility of the time. We have already seen how Margaret Paston tried to defend the property here. The rise of the Pastons from their Norfolk obscurity began with William Paston, a lawyer who made a good marriage and became a Judge of Common Pleas in 1429. It was he who purchased lands including the manor of Gresham. His son John inherited the extensive properties of Sir John Fastolf (Shakespeare's Falstaff), principal among which was Caister Castle, by a will which was much disputed. The consequences of this gave rise to a large part of the correspondence, John's wife Margaret keeping her husband well informed of proceedings during his frequent absences in London. Their two eldest sons, both named John, were knighted in due course, and the family slowly rose in wealth and influence until in the seventeenth century Robert Paston was created Baron Paston and Viscount Yarmouth, only to have all his titles and estates lost by his son William, whose three sons all died before him.

The sort of life revealed by the vast fifteenth-century correspondence of the family was probably typical of most rural landowners of the period. Their letters are overwhelmingly concerned with their territorial rights. They were not inclined to tell sad stories of the death of kings, except in so far as national affairs touched their own welfare. There is no mention of music or painting, nor of the invention of printing from movable types, or the discovery of America. They were literate but not cultured. I dare say the Pastons who were contemporaries of Copernicus could not have cared less whether the world were flat or square, so long as their citadels remained intact. Their concerns were as they must have been with most men of property in that unsettled period – the security and management of their various manors; bargaining for good marriages for their womenfolk; frequent shopping lists for goods that could be obtained more easily in London than in Norfolk; occasional reluctance to send money by servants lest they should be robbed on the road; gossip about women between brothers. Though they had risen from humble beginnings themselves, it was not long before they were so put out when one of their number, Margery, was betrothed to Richard Calle, a bailiff, that they disowned her.

The period was one when more ordinary people were becoming literate. In 1476 John Paston, recommending a clerk to William, Lord Hastings, said that the man was 'well spoken in English, meekly well in French, and very perfect in Flemish. He can write and read.' Bailiffs were able to keep careful accounts, and one of them advised Agnes Paston in 1435 that he had let for fifteen shillings a place of hers that was in a bad state of repair: '. . . the locks of the doors are pulled off and borne away, and the windows be broken and gone, and other boards be nailed on in the stead of the said windows. Also, the swine-stye is down, and all the timber and the thatch born away; also the hedge is broken or borne away, which closed the garden; wherethrough the place is evil appeyred to the tenant.'

It was necessary to keep the bailiffs on their toes, however, as John Paston makes clear in a letter to his wife giving instructions about what was to be done during his absence,

> as well for provision of stuff for mine household as for the gathering of the revenue of my livelode or grains, or for setting a-work of my servants, and for the more politic means of selling and carrying of my malt, and for all other things necessary for to be done; and that when I come home I have not an excuse, saying that he spoke to my servants, and that . . . they were so busy they might not attend. For I will have my matter so guided that if any man may not attend another shall be commanded to do it; and if my servants fail, I had lever wage some other man, for a journey or a season, than my matter should be unsped.

It was only three or four years after the first John Paston's death, however, that his second son had to advise his heir that unless he carried out hasty repairs at Caister, the job would cost him double, 'for the rain hath so moistened the walls in many places that they may not tile the houses till the walls be repaired, or else ye shall have double cost for to untile your houses again at such as ye shall amend the walls. And if it be not done this year, many of the walls will lie in the moat ere long. . . .'

Huge numbers of moated sites have been traced – more than two thousand throughout Britain – often nowadays without buildings on them. A large majority of them probably enclosed manor houses of the late Middle Ages, when any self-respecting lord of the manor might require a moat to set his house apart from the vulgar masses. Since moats are best suited to clay soils, it has been suggested that there was more to digging a moat, even in those later medieval times, than just its value as a status symbol. The clay areas were where bricks came into earliest use in the absence of building stone, and the excavation of a moat would at the same time provide clay for the bricks which in those days were made on the building sites by itinerant craftsmen.

This would have been the case at Oxburgh in Norfolk, and also at Herstmonceux Castle in Sussex, but it was not so at Tattershall Castle in Lincolnshire, for although this house is moated, it is known that Ralph Cromwell, who built it around 1440, had the bricks made ten miles away under the supervision of a German brickmaker.

Nor was it the case at Baddesley Clinton, in Warwickshire, where the principal material is stone, though much brickwork was added in later centuries. The original house with its moat was built by the Bromes, who married into that prospering family we first met at Oakham Castle, the Ferrers, who held the property from 1517, when Nicholas Brome died, until 1884. The wide moat, the battlemented porch and the presence of arrow-slits might lead one to think that defence was very much on the minds of the builders here, but the battlements were added in the nineteenth century, as was so much else here at other times, but the overall picture is still that of a house built for stylish living.

The Ferrers were Catholics, and during the Tudor religious hostilities good use was made of the drainage system built into the house. A tunnel, 2½ feet wide, was built beneath the house as a sewer. Slots in its roof received the domestic drainage and carried it to the moat, and it could be cleaned out by raising the moat's water level. This tunnel became a hiding-place for Catholic priests, who stooped up to their ankles in water for hours whilst the house was being searched by zealous priest-hunters. The Jesuit Father Gerard was among those who hid there.

At Great Chalfield, in Wiltshire, the material is buff limestone. Here is one of the finest late-medieval manor houses surviving in Britain. It was built by Sir Thomas Tropenell, who acquired the manor in 1467 after fifteen years of legal wrangling. He and his successors made it into a classic manorial nucleus, for he built the church near the house, and both are reached via a stone bridge across the moat and a gatehouse, while a mill, barn and various outbuildings are in close proximity. The house itself is

Great Chalfield Manor, Wiltshire, from the south

built round a courtyard. Part of the original house has disappeared, and what remains has been much restored, having fallen into a bad state in the nineteenth century. But the façade of the house as one turns to it from the gatehouse must be very much as Tropenell built it.

The great hall is in the centre of this H-plan house, with the two-storey gabled porch on the right and a symmetrically positioned window projection on the left, adjoining taller gables at each end of the cross-wings, which both have oriel windows, the one on the left being in the solar and the one on the right in what was presumably a bedroom. Carved stone figures of soldiers, and griffins holding the Tropenell arms, stand on the gable ends.

One enters the hall through the screens passage, the carved wooden screen being a nineteenth-century copy of the original one. The screen here, however, did not hide the doorways to kitchen, buttery and pantry, as was usual, but to a dining-room, which is perhaps the earliest surviving in England. Langland has 'Piers Plowman' complaining about the growing anti-social practice of dining apart, in the preceding century, saying that the hall, which was made for meals, was a wretched place as a result:

> There the lord and lady liketh not to sit;
> Now have the rich a rule to eat by themselves
> In a privy parlour. . . .

The privy parlour would probably at first have been the room below the solar at the high table end of the hall, but here at Great Chalfield it was specially built at the opposite end, displacing the customary service rooms from their time-honoured location. Three squints of rare design look into the hall. Two of them give views from the rooms above the bays in the hall, and the other from the gallery above the screens passage. All of them have stone faces with hollow eyes and mouths. One is a bishop, and another is King Midas with his ass ears, and all three wear appropriately cynical expressions, reminding us that, although Henry Tudor occupied the throne by the time Sir Thomas Tropenell died, and the ancient manorial system was virtually extinct, old feudal habits died hard, and the lord of the manor still had power and influence over his tenants and retainers which he exercised without scruple. The overriding impression at Great Chalfield, however, is of a lord and his family devoted to good living in a house of style, with no concern about defence.

Only a few miles away from the field of battle where Richard III lost his kingdom and his life is Appleby Magna, where another moated manor house of the mid-fifteenth century must have presented a picture of peace and comfort to the world, despite its fairly formidable gatehouse. It had a laver, or wash-basin, hollowed out of a solid block of stone, with a pipe running from the bottom for drainage. The Appleby family had been here for four hundred years when they sold the place in 1560, but their house was replaced by the half-timbered building we see there now, and the moat is but a poor relic of its former self.

Little Moreton Hall in Cheshire, by contrast, seems in pristine condition, as if it were built only yesterday, and this splendidly exuberant structure of black and white timber framing is de-servedly among the best-known manor houses in the country. It is visible from all sides in the flat local countryside, and defence was never seriously in the minds of the Moreton family when they built the 'little' great hall and its adjoining rooms on one side of the cobbled courtyard, around 1480. The front range was not built for another hundred years, but since the building has undergone very little alteration, and although the most spectacular part of the house is Elizabethan, with fine leaded glass windows, the place belongs in this chapter as an instance of the late-medieval island mansion. It, too, had its priest-holes, as well as its garderobes discharging into the moat. It also had a long gallery, built on top in the second half of the sixteenth century, and crazily quaint bay windows. Each floor going upwards seems to overhang the one below as if to disprove all laws of stability, not to mention gravity, and the whole tipsy assembly is a bit like a bag of old-fashioned humbugs all stuck together.

One of the oldest surviving houses in Hertfordshire is the fine gabled manor house called Lordship House, near the church in the delightful village of Cottered. It is a farmhouse now and was altered in the seventeenth century, but it stands on the moated site where it was built not long after the Black Death had devastated the village and perhaps also Broadfield, nearby, a lost village where the original manor house seems to have been demolished in 1220 to make way for a church, itself destroyed soon after the visitation of the plague.

Salisbury Hall was built by Henry VIII's Treasurer, Sir John Cuttes, on a site that was already moated in Norman times. The house was modernized in the late seventeenth century, but it had been visited several times by Charles II, and legend has it that Nell Gwynne stayed in the lodge near by, one day desperately holding her first child by Charles over the moat and threatening to drop him in if he were not granted a title, whereupon the Merry Monarch is supposed to have cried: 'Nelly, Nelly, don't kill the Duke of St Albans!' The later house's occupants have included Lady Randolph Churchill and the railway engineer Sir Nigel Gresley.

The village of Thorley, near Bishop's Stortford, has an ancient manor house, much modernized in the eighteenth century, after which it declined to farmhouse status, but it has traces of a moat and the remains of an aisled great hall of the fourteenth century which – so local tradition has it – was owned by Richard Whittington, the well-known cat-fancier and thrice Lord Mayor of London. Leventhorpes and Rapers were among later lords of this manor, and at the beginning of the nineteenth century, it was held up for a time by Lord Ellenborough, a throw-back to medieval tyranny, for he was known as the 'hanging judge' and made a solemn speech in 1810 to warn the nation that if the death

penalty for shoplifting were abolished, every man who set foot out of doors for an hour would be liable to find his house emptied of every vestige of his property when he returned.

In Worcestershire, Birtsmorton Court, west of Tewkesbury, is a picturesque moated house of several periods but originated from the fourteenth century and having a few remains from that time. It is built of stone and timber-framing and stands in a wide moat crossed by a stone bridge. It was reputed to be a refuge of Sir John Oldcastle, when Henry VI presented the manor to his Esquire of the Body, John Nanfan, and the Nanfans also gave refuge here to Thomas Wolsey, an ambitious young man who had fallen foul of Sir Amyas Paulet of Hinton St George in Somerset. He had the young Wolsey put in the stocks for some misdemeanour. Wolsey duly became chaplain to Sir Richard Nanfan, who recommended him to Henry VII, and many years later, when it was Wolsey himself whom people needed refuge from, the Cardinal took his long-awaited revenge on Paulet by having him confined in the Middle Temple.

The house was owned at one time by the Hakluyt family, to which the geographer Richard Hakluyt belonged, but the Nanfans were the longest survivors here, and they made many alterations to the old house, which eventually passed by a series of marriages to William Huskisson. His son, the MP and – so many thought – a future Prime Minister, was born here and became an early victim of the age of the train, being run over and killed by Stephenson's *Rocket* at the opening of the Manchester and Liverpool Railway.

Nether Hall in Essex was once a fine moated manor house of brick, built by Thomas Colte in 1470 and held by his family for nearly two hundred years. But the house fell into ruin, and its materials were plundered to build modern houses, the remains of the old manor house being left standing in the middle of a farmyard from the late eighteenth century onwards. The gate-house and parts of the curtain wall remain, with a brick staircase from the time of Thomas Colte, whose monument is in the village church at Roydon.

At Crowhurst, Surrey (not to be confused with the previously mentioned Crowhurst in Sussex), a barrister, John Gaynesford, became lord of the manor around 1425 and built himself a fine moated half-timbered house with many gables. It had a small hall of only two bays but with good carpentry in the roof, a screens passage with three service doorways, and a withdrawing-room at the opposite end. The Gaynesfords occupied the

The long gallery at Little Moreton Hall, Cheshire

house until 1699, but it then fell into farmhouse use until it was purchased in 1724 by Sarah, Duchess of Marlborough, who restored it and used the rents to finance her almshouses at St Albans. At the end of the nineteenth century it passed again into the Gainsford family and was in due course leased to none other than the then Duchess of Marlborough by George Crawley, an architect who restored the old house, as Pevsner says, 'out of all recognition' after the First World War, making it a much bigger house and giving it, among other things, a stone dovecote and many mock-Tudor details.

Despite the fashion in the fifteenth century for moats, not all lords of the manor had them. Many perhaps did not want them, and many more, no doubt, could ill afford them. Rufford Old Hall in Lancashire was in process of building not far away from Little Moreton Hall at more or less the same time, and there can hardly be any question whether the Heskeths could have afforded a moat if they had fancied one. The great hall is a spectacular timber structure, with hammer beams and angels. There is also a rare survival here of what is whimsically called a movable screen. The heavy oak frame alone is seven feet high, and that is surmounted by three huge carved pinnacles as high again, so that even if the thing were on castors (which it is not), moving it would be like moving the sight-screen on a cricket ground single-handed. At the other end of the hall, a coved canopy had an ingenious priests' hole behind it. Apart from the great hall, most of Rufford is work of the seventeenth century and later.

We have jumped a lot in time and space in looking at the moated manor houses together, and Littlehempston, in Devon, takes us back to the beginning of the fifteenth century. This was a small house compared with Rufford, and indeed with Dartington, which is quite near, but it is attractive in its simplicity, and during its career it has been a nunnery and a rectory as well as a manor house, but it is in peaceful country and was designed for simple comforts.

Bradley Manor, once called Highweek Manor, is on the outskirts of Newton Abbot, surprisingly quiet in a little valley, and although there are traces of a thirteenth-century house here, the present building dates from 1419, when it was begun by the Yarde family. The gabled front with its oriel windows was not completed until the end of the century, but the great hall with its accompanying rooms and chapel are the original work, the ground-floor chapel having a high chancel with

Rufford Old Hall, Lancashire, with fine roof and movable screen

Bradley Manor, Devon

a four-centred barrel roof and carved bosses, and a traceried window.

Another gabled manor house of similar date is Bindon, near the county's border with Dorset. The chapel was licensed in 1425, but this building qualifies as a tower house like that at Shute not far away and may have earlier origins with security in mind at first. It had comfort as its priority by the fifteenth century, however, and among its furnishings are three decorated fireplaces and a carved piscina in the chapel.

Rymans (not to be confused with Nymans) at Appledram or Apuldram in West Sussex near Chichester is also a tower house of sorts, but here again there can be no doubt that comfort and style were the principal concerns of the builder, William Ryman, who began the house in the second decade of the century and was evidently very fussy about the material used, having had limestone brought here from France and the Isle of Wight. The stone from Caen, in Normandy, had been used in English church building in the south-east since the Norman Conquest, not only for political reasons but also because it was as cheap to transport the stone by sea from Normandy as to carry native stone by land from inland quarries. Ryman had his solar or great chamber on the first floor with parlour below and bedroom above, and in a wing forming an L-shape with the tower block was the great hall, whilst another wing was probably built as an office where the owner conducted his manorial business. The house had built-in garderobes, and the upper floors were reached by the usual spiral staircase.

At about the same time as the Suffolks were building their red brick ensemble at Ewelme in the Oxfordshire Chilterns, another man of power and wealth, William Lovell, the seventh baron of that name, was building a manor house of limestone at Minster Lovell, on the county's Cotswold fringe, the family having owned the manor since the twelfth century. There are traces of a moat here, but the manor house, on the site of a Norman priory, was not built for defence. It stood beside the River Windrush among trees in a picturesque landscape and was on the scale of a palace. It is now, alas, in ruins, but we can see its layout and imagine the life that went on here in contrast to the more modest living in those smaller manor houses which form the bulk of survivals from this period.

The lofty great hall was on the north side of a large courtyard, with solar and chapel adjacent to it on the upper floor. The hall had large Perpendicular windows high up its walls. A wing along the east side of the courtyard contained the pantry, buttery and kitchen and was terminated by the stables. The west wing reached almost to the river bank and had several private and guest rooms with wall fireplaces. The kitchen also had a large wall fireplace, but the hall had none, a central hearth apparently being used, with openings at the top of the walls to withdraw the smoke instead of a louvre in the roof. The central hearth had by no means died out. It persisted well into Tudor times, and its eventual passing was mourned by Rev. William Harrison, among others, for he wrote that 'our tenderlings complaine of rheumes, catarhs, and poses. Then we had none

Tracery in a surviving window of Minster Lovell Hall, Oxfordshire

but reredoses, and our heads did never ache. For as the smoke of those daies was supposed to be a sufficient hardning of the timber of the houses, so it was reputed to be a far better medicine to keep the good man and his family.' It seems likely that it was considered fit only for the servants by this time, however.

A well in the courtyard supplied water to a stone tank, installed after the Lovells had departed. A lavatory pit at the end of the west wing drained into the river. A large circular dovecote was built nearby, the birds being used to train the lord's falcons, no doubt, as well as to supply his table with meat. Lord Lovell also had a hunting park in Wychwood Forest, where the villagers were allowed to graze their horses and cattle.

William Lovel died in 1455, and his son John ten years after him. The property passed to William's grandson Francis, the ninth baron, who probably built the tower at the south-west corner of the courtyard, when times were a little more hazardous, especially for someone as widely hated as he was, whom the Lancastrians named openly in the seditious couplet which also clearly identified Richard III and his other cronies, Catesby and Ratcliffe:

> The Cat, the Rat, and Lovel our Dog,
> Rule all England under an Hog.

William Colyngbourne, the Wiltshire squire who had his provocative lampoon fixed to the door of St Paul's Cathedral, was brought to trial before a court of which Lord Lovel was a member, but the rhyme was not Colyngbourne's sole offence, for he had evidently been an agent of Henry Tudor and had sent a message to the Welshman urging him to land in England with an army. Colyngbourne was duly convicted of treason and was hanged, and disembowelled while still living.

Lovel, meanwhile, prospered, and fought with Richard at Bosworth, but when the King was killed, Lovel escaped. He may have been Richard's friend from childhood, but the days were long gone when a man should die beside his lord – even if his lord was the king – so Lovel went into hiding and emerged again later in support of the rebellion by Lambert Simnel. What became of him after that abortive escapade is not known for certain, but dark legends drift like fog round the ruins of Minster Lovell Hall. It is said that Lovel made his way home and hid in a vault, known only to one loyal old retainer who kept the key and brought him food and drink. But the servant died suddenly, and Lovel was entombed alive.

In 1708, the Clerk of the House of Commons reported that workmen carrying out repairs at the hall had discovered a secret room in which the skeletons of a man and a dog had been seen before they crumbled to dust in the fresh air. The man had been seated at a table with papers and a book on it. This is one of those macabre stories that we all like to shiver at and believe, but it must be treated with scepticism, as there is no proof of the workmen's story. Besides, the property had been confiscated smartly from the Lovels by Henry VII. Nevertheless, the ghost of

Francis Lovel is said to haunt the place. After various leases, the manor was bought by Sir Edward Coke in 1602, and it was Thomas Coke, Earl of Leicester, who dismantled the house when he went to live at Holkham Hall in Norfolk. The ruins were then used as farm buildings for many years, before being res- · cued and protected by the Ministry of Works.

A contemporary of William Lovel was Ralph Cromwell, Lord Treasurer to Henry VI, and it was he who began the building of another of the great manor houses of England at South Wingfield in Derbyshire. This also is now a ruin of dark stone. Cromwell acquired the manor in 1440. As well as being the King's exchequer, he was also his Master of Hounds and Falcons and Warden of Sherwood Forest, and he set about building a house befitting his great wealth and importance, but he died in 1455 before it was completed. It was finished by John Talbot, Earl of Shrewsbury, to whom the manor passed on Cromwell's death, and it was little altered afterwards. The Talbots and their successors lived at Wingfield for nearly two hundred years, until the Civil War, when the process of decay began with partial demolition by a better-known Cromwell – a nice irony. It is arguable that this house belongs in the previous chapter, for it was unquestionably provided with some defensive features, having a strong four-storey tower and a fortified gateway, where the double purse badge of the Lord Treasurer is carved in stone. The proper comforts of a rich and powerful lord of the manor dictated the scale and layout of Wingfield, however, and although the great hall is on the upper floor, over a very fine vaulted undercroft, this was an architectural necessity rather than a defensive measure, since the manor was built on sloping ground.

The hall was a large one by manor house standards – seventy-two by thirty-seven feet. This is almost as big in floor area as Oakham Castle's hall, though longer and narrower. The solar, screens and passage and service rooms were on the classic pattern, and the place was well supplied with wall fireplaces and hung with tapestries. One would have thought that Mary, Queen of Scots, would have been quite comfortable here during her several visits in custody, but on two occasions she fell ill here, and the physician sent by the Privy Council criticized the sanitary conditions, to which the Earl of Shrewsbury replied that it was the 'continued festering and uncleanly order' of her own retinue which was damaging her health. He must have been pleased to be rid of her in the end, for his jealous wife, Bess of

Lytes Cary, the manor house in Somerset

Hardwick, had spread ugly rumours about his relationship with his prisoner.

No such domestic emotions seem to have upset the lord and lady of the manor at Lytes Cary, in Somerset, where we see carved horses and swans everywhere – swans being the heraldic emblems of John Lyte, whose family had been here since the thirteenth century, and horses those of his wife, Edith Horsey – presumably a dreadful medieval pun. The house has a splendidly impressive façade. The chapel dates from the fourteenth century, but the great hall is of the first half of the next, and it has a fine timber ceiling and a large wall fireplace, as well as an oriel chamber where, once again, the lord's family may have dined separately from the rest of the household, for it was John Lyte who added this room in the sixteenth century, complete with its own fireplace. A spiral staircase led from hall to solar. The Lyte family spread far and wide from their early medieval beginnings here and left more of themselves than their homes – one of them wrote the hymns 'Abide With Me' and 'Praise, my soul, the King of Heaven', while an earlier member wrote a *Niewe Herball*.

Gardening has been at the forefront of the Lloyd family's interests, too, as can readily be seen at their home at Great Dixter, East Sussex. Much of this house is the modern work of Lutyens, but the original fifteenth-century hall survives, with its timber roof alternating tie-beams and hammer-beams.

At Ordsall Hall, in Salford, Greater Manchester, the spectacular half-timbering is all original fifteenth-century craftsmanship and ten thousand miles away from Coronation Street in its stylishness and dignity, despite the fact that the north-western

The great hall at Ordsall, with its central hearth

taste for external show is evident here. The usual three doors to the service rooms from the screens passage are present at one end of the hall, and a coved canopy was over the high table, as at Rufford. This house is now preserved as a museum, and one should not be deterred by the ugly Victorian side of the place which one approaches first.

Ashleworth, north of Gloucester, presents us with something of a problem. At the centre of this attractive village by the Severn, the church stands in a group with a house called 'The Court' and a tithe barne, whilst nearby is 'Ashleworth Manor' built about the same time as the Court (1460) and by the same

Ockwells Manor, Berkshire – the garden front

person – Abbot Newbury of Bristol. Which, if either of these, is a manor house? David Verey, in the *Buildings of England*, repeats the story that Ashleworth Manor was built as a summer residence, and it is indeed the Court which was the manor house, the so-called Manor having become a vicarage in due course. The manor house was built of Jurassic limestone and was originally thatched but is now tiled, the hall having been subdivided horizontally to form an upper room where the original roof timbers survive. A circular staircase of stone led to the solar.

Nothing could form a greater contrast with this house of Cotswold stone than the timber-framed splendour of Ockwells in Berkshire. It was built by Sir John Norreys in the middle of the fifteenth century, in what was then a secluded corner of the county near Maidenhead. He was Master of the Wardrobe to Henry VI and Esquire of the Body to both Henry and his successor Edward IV. The house was only just complete when he died in 1467, for in his will of 1465 he referred to the house as 'not yet finished'. The Norreys family were ardent royalists. Indeed, one of them loved royalty so much that he was accused

and executed as one of those who had slept with the Queen,
Anne Boleyn, when the King was casting around desperately for
an excuse to be rid of her. But the pride of the family in their court
connections is clearly signified at Ockwells, where the main
façade, like that at Great Chalfield, is formed by double gables –
the outer ones higher than the inner – flanking the great hall.
There the resemblance ends, however, for in place of the solid
stonework of the Wiltshire manor house, the Berkshire one
consists of elaborately carved timber and much glass, with
patterned brick infilling. The solar is in the usual position at the
high table end of the hall, but the buttery, pantry and kitchen
were separate from the hall block, being across a small courtyard
with a cloister between. Perhaps here we see for the first time the
writing on the wall for the great hall as the nucleus of the manor
house, although here the hall is fine enough, if a modest size,
with a stone wall fireplace.

What is most impressive about Ockwells, however, is the
glass. It was still relatively luxurious at this time, but the house is
full of it, with eighteen shields of armorial stained glass in the
hall, the arms including those of Henry VI and Margaret of
Anjou, Sir John Wenlock, Margaret's Keeper of the Wardrobe,
whom Norrys appointed his executor; and Norrys's nephew
Richard Bulstrode, who became Edward IV's Comptroller of the
Household. This fine glass was probably made by John Prudde
of Eton, the King's Chief Glazier, and the wealth of other glass in
the multitudinous windows of this light-drenched manor
house make it a sort of medieval crystal palace.

There is a brass to William Norrys, who died in 1591, in the
church at Bray, where the lord of the manor would no doubt
have been on familiar terms with the famed vicar who changed
his religion as often as was necessary to retain his living. By this
time, however, the Norrys clan had married into the Williams
family and acquired the lordship of Rycote in Oxfordshire,
where Queen Elizabeth visited them twice. Alas, the manor
house here has entirely disappeared, having been demolished
after a disastrous fire. At Ockwells, the Norryses were succeeded by the Fettiplaces, who also held the ancient Appleton
Manor which we noticed in the second chapter, among their
other lands extending into fifteen counties.

Elizabeth's standard-bearer lived at Pattyndenne Manor at
Goudhurst, Kent – a timber-framed house built in 1470 on a
classic local pattern, with one roof covering the great hall and
two wings which project slightly. The roof timbers are now in an

Gainsborough Old Hall, Lincolnshire

upper room, the hall having since been sub-divided, but they can be seen quite clearly and are richly carved.

Of similar date, but totally dissimilar in style, is Gainsborough Old Hall in Lincolnshire. Legend has it that the house stands on the site of the Saxon palace where Alfred the Great married Ealswythe. The manor house is a tall, partly timbered and partly brick building with steeply pitched roof and a forest of chimneys, and it looks from one angle – particularly in its present environment – more like a factory than a manor house, and in fact it was used as such from the middle of the eighteenth century, and then as a ballroom later. Nevertheless, it was built by the Yorkist Sir Thomas Burgh, whose previous house had been burnt down by the Lancastrians, and Richard III visited Burgh's son, also Sir Thomas, here in 1484.

Brick oriels on the chimneyed wing contained lavatory chambers. The hall is quite large and has a fine arch-braced roof, with a bay window at the high table end, with a carved stone lion. At the other end, the doors to the service rooms remain, and the kitchen itself is one of the best survivals of the period, with two

Selly Manor on its original site at Selly Oak. A photograph of 1898

huge fireplaces and a high timber roof. It is claimed that Henry VIII met the twice-widowed Catherine Parr here, for she had been married to Sir Edward Burgh first, and then to Lord Latymer, and was still only thirty-one when she was married to the King. He preceded her to the grave like her previous husbands, leaving her time to marry yet again.

Towards the end of Queen Elizabeth's reign, the manor of Gainsborough was purchased from the Burgh family by William Hickman, and the house became a sort of rendezvous for Protestant thinkers from Bishop Hooper and John Foxe to John Robinson, pastor of the Pilgrim Fathers, and later John Wesley, who 'preached at Gainsborough in Sir Nevil Hickman's great hall'. As might be expected, the dreary modern town in which it stands is well supplied with Nonconformist chapels.

At Bournville, two ancient manor houses which once stood in Warwickshire villages, when Birmingham itself was no more than a tiny dot on the map of England, were dismantled and re-erected in their new model village by the Cadbury family early in this century. George Cadbury bought Selly Manor in

1907, when it was scheduled for demolition, and moved it from its original site near Selly Oak, using as much of the original timber, brick and other fabric as was possible. The house was originally built in the fourteenth century but had been much altered later, brick infilling in herringbone pattern having replaced the original lath and plaster in the Tudor period, when the chimneys were also built. The house, which became three tenements at a later stage in its life, has a jettied gable on one wing, and a spiral staircase with timber newel posts.

Also near Bournville's village green is the manor house of Minworth Greaves. This was re-erected between 1929 and 1932, having likewise been saved from destruction, although it was in such a sorry condition that no more than the timber-framing and roof trusses of the great hall could be re-used. The hall, however, is of cruck construction and dates in all probability from the fourteenth century.

At the south-east corner of Leicestershire, in quiet countryside little frequented by tourists, is Nevill Holt, a small place consisting of hall, church and a few houses. A village called Holt stood here once on the high ground overlooking the Welland valley. It was largely depopulated at some stage, for what reason we cannot be sure, but probably in the course of creating a park for the big house. It was the Palmer family who built the original house in the fifteenth century, and some details of it remain, in particular the oriel window of 1476 built by Sir Thomas Palmer, with much ornamental stone carving of men and animals, delightful tracery between the tall mullions, and a battlemented top.

In the sixteenth century the estate passed to the Nevill family through the marriage of William Nevill with the Palmer heiress, and it was the Nevills who enlarged the house and in all probability depopulated the village, since when the estate has been known as Nevill Holt. It was Sir Thomas Nevill who added a fine stone porch to the house, and a spiral staircase in the hall leads to the room in the porch over the entrance, having previously led to the minstrels' gallery over the screens passage. The hall has an open timber roof, but much Jacobean work has changed the medieval character of the house inside, not to mention the more modern alterations.

The direct line of descent of the Nevills ceased in 1728, when the last daughter of the family was married to an Italian count, and in the same year medicinal waters were discovered there, which Countess Migliorucci seems to have exploited with some enthusiasm at first. A Dr Thomas Short of Sheffield waxed eloquent in its praises, claiming it as an infallible cure-all, but Nevill Holt did not last long as a spa, the sensible folk of Leicestershire and Rutland doubtless finding the doctor's testimonials to be exaggerated, as well as vague: 'The effect this water had on a clergyman's daughter was really wonderful, etc.'

The Cunard family occupied the manor house for nearly fifty years, and it was then sold to Rev. C. A. C. Bowlker in 1919. He turned it into a school for boys, and it has remained as such, now being a branch of the famous Uppingham School.

A little to the east of Chippenham, in Wiltshire, is Sheldon Manor, a stone house dating partly from the fifteenth century and standing among old barns and older yew trees, with a detached contemporary chapel. The mullioned and transomed windows are later additions, and the house's two-storey gabled porch, of the late thirteenth century (i.e. remaining from an earlier house and looking a bit too big for this one), was built by the lord of the manor Sir Geoffrey Gascelyn. The modern house's gardens are noted for their fine old-fashioned roses.

South Wraxall Manor is a very successful blending of Tudor and Jacobean stylishness and comfort with a more modest house of the fifteenth-century lords of the manor, the Long family whose memorials populate the village church and who made their fortunes in the clothing trade. What became the manor farmhouse, close by, was originally a hospice for poor travellers in these parts, built in the fourteenth century and consisting of hall and chapel. It was Sir Robert Long who built the medieval part of the big house, probably on the site of an older one. It is of irregular plan and built of the local mellow limestone, with a fine gatehouse, and gargoyles on its two-storey porch. The porch is at the screens end of the great hall and is balanced at the other end by a projecting chimney breast and an oriel window. This house was built for comfort, and when Sir Walter Long expanded it in the Elizabethan period, his architect, though more flamboyant, designed it in sympathy with the older work so that the whole is now undoubtedly among the most attractive of ancient manor houses in England. Yet it has much to answer for. In the house is a so-called Raleigh Room, and the story is that here the two Sir Walters were the first men in England to smoke tobacco. Whether the story is true or not that one of Sir Walter Long's servants drenched Raleigh with water believing him to be on fire, one wishes his light could have been extinguished there and then, for ever.

Westwood Manor has parts dating from as early as 1400, but the late fifteenth and early sixteenth centuries were the main building periods of this house where the manor belonged first to Thomas Culverhouse and then to Thomas Horton. Even later, much Jacobean work was done on it, and the old hall was sub-divided to make a great chamber above, so that there is relatively little now that can be attributed to the late medieval period, although a fine stone barn of the fifteenth century remains to form a manorial nucleus with the parish church, partly rebuilt by Thomas Horton. At length the house became a farmhouse until it was rescued and presented to the National Trust.

As we move towards the Tudor expansion of the next chapter, we find a crop of late medieval manor houses in south-west England, but before we go in that direction, two other survivals of the end of the fifteenth century call for attention, one in Essex and the other in Cheshire.

At Hockey, in Essex, Sir John Cuttle, who was to become Henry VIII's Treasurer of the Household, started to build the manor house called Horham Hall in 1502 but left it still un-finished when he died eighteen years later. There had been a timber-framed house on the site before, which had a moat. The new house was built of brick with stone dressings. The original timber roof of the hall is hidden by a ceiling, but there is a louvre opening in it, indicating the former presence of a central hearth, even at this late date, with a lantern on the roof.

Adlington Hall, in Cheshire, has much Tudor and later build-ing, with parts of brick, stone and timber, but the great hall here is of the house built by 1505, the lord of the manor being one of the Legh family who had been here since the early fourteenth century and who are still here now. The hall has a hammerbeam roof, and its date is on the canopy at the high table end. One of the curiosities here is a fine seventeenth-century organ on which Handel is said to have played. He may well have done, for he was certainly a guest of the Leghs, although that powerful local family of landowners had been noted more for its fighting qualities than for its patronage of the arts.

Towards the south-west, we might pause in the Cotswolds, where Little Sodbury has a manor house with great hall surviv-ing from late in the fifteenth century. Most of the rest of the house is Tudor and later work. The young William Tyndale taught the sons of Sir John Walshe here in Henry VIII's time. The great hall's roof has braced collar-beams, wind-braces and

moulded purlins, and the two-storey porch contains steps leading up at right angles to the main building, and both the porch
and the room above it have squints overlooking the gate. One
squint here has a carved face – the only one of its kind known
apart from those at Great Chalfield.

Two late-medieval manor houses of importance survive in
Somerset, at Cothay and Gothelney. Cothay was probably the
earlier of the two, though only by a little, and it is described by
Pevsner as 'one of the most perfect smaller English manor
houses of the late C15'. It stands near the River Tone, set among
the folds of the hills close to the Devon border, and was built by
the Bluett family, lords of the manor from the mid-fourteenth
century, but absentee landlords until Walter Bluett built this
house and lived here from about 1480. The family coat of arms is
on the gateway, in a battlemented tower, and there is a brass to
Walter's son Richard and his wife in the parish church at
Kittisford, across the river. The gatehouse opens onto a small
green with a large pond before it, and the old stone house with
its gables and mullioned and transomed windows stands across
a lawn as an image of serenity.

Although relatively small, Cothay has all the classic features of
the medieval manor house – hall with screens passage, spiral
staircase, solar, dining-room, parlour and private chapel
reached via a gallery at the screens passage end of the hall. It is a
significant sign of the times, perhaps, that the solar is almost the
same size as the hall, and the staircase no longer leads direct
from hall to solar but is more conveniently placed for the private
dining-room. There is another interesting detail about the staircase. It ascends in an anti-clockwise direction. The time had
passed when space was needed for the sword-arm. Much addition was done at Cothay in the seventeenth century, but the
original screen and timber roof remain in the hall, and in the
solar there are roof timbers similar to those in the hall. The
minstrels' gallery was a feature which was just beginning to
come into fashion at about this time. The Bluetts were clearly
what might now be called 'with it'. Fifteenth-century wall paintings survive here also – among the oldest remaining in secular
domestic buildings, though some of them are religious in character. Although the house has served its time as a farmhouse,
having been let to tenants by the Bluetts, who still owned the
place well into the Victorian era, it remains one of the best
surviving manor houses of its time.

Gothelney is not so well documented, nor as well preserved,

The great hall at Horham Hall, Essex

but it dates from about 1500 and is interesting mainly because its hall seems to have been built right from the start with a ceiling to form another large room above it. Thick walls enclose this tall structure. The porch and a garderobe were built in the same projection at the front centre of the house, the porch leading into the screens passage with the hall to the left and kitchen and buttery to the right, and a spiral staircase at the back which here, too, ascended in anti-clockwise direction. A brass in the floor of the church at Charlinch is to Jasper Bourne, who was lord of the manor here in the seventeenth century.

Halsway Manor is less important but still interesting, not least for its picturesque siting on the Quantock slopes. The lords of the manor here in the fifteenth century were the Stradling family, who built their house of red sandstone rubble, with battlements and pinnacles, along a village lane at Crowcombe, where Cardinal Beaufort had had a hunting-lodge not long before. In the late nineteenth century, half the house was rebuilt in ashlar and the interior remodelled, with panelling and furnishings imported from various sources, so that the medieval remains have to be sought out in a house now devoted to the study of folk music.

Cornwall presents us with three notable examples of late-medieval manor houses built as Middle Age England waned and the advent of the Tudors heralded changes in architecture as in so much else, so that buildings in the old styles were either rebuilt or allowed to decay. Ebbingford Manor is a stone house with medieval, Tudor and Georgian elements. It stands at Bude, on the west bank of the Bude and Holsworthy Canal, which of course did not exist when the Arundells built their manor house here. The canal is now one subject of the exhibition of local history in the house. The Arundells owned it until the eighteenth century, after which it was much restored by the new owner, having the date 1758 on a stone tablet.

Rialton is in the parish of St Columb Minor and was a monastic manor of the monks of St Petroc at Bodmin. It was built late in the fifteenth century and has first-floor rooms where the Prior of Bodmin used to stay. But then came the Dissolution and gradual desecration, the house with its battlemented porch and three-light windows becoming a farmhouse, its great hall sub-divided, though the original wagon roof is still there. The Duchy of Cornwall owns the estate today.

Trecarrel, south of Launceston, has fared even worse, being at one time not even a farmhouse but only a barn. It was built by Sir

Henry Trecarrel around the turn of the Tudor century. It had a fine hall, with cradle roof and dais, and mullioned and transomed windows with Perpendicular tracery. There was a detached private chapel, which is still intact, and a priest's room above it with a fireplace and garderobe. It is said that Sir Henry was building a new wing to what he intended as a large house when his only child was accidentally drowned in its bath, and he then devoted himself to religion instead, giving Launceston church what Pevsner calls its 'barbarous profuseness' of external decoration.

In Dorset, Purse Caundle and Athelhampton manors just preceded the Tudor dynasty. Purse Caundle is part of that diadem of golden limestone crowning the lovely town of Sherborne, and its manor house was known locally as 'King John's House' at one time, though rather late for that popular attribution, unless there was something earlier here that we are not aware of. This is quite likely, as the house is said to be haunted by the sounds of a hunting-horn and hounds, which might relate to a royal bailiff who killed a white deer in the valley and enraged Henry III so much that he imposed a local tax called White Hart Silver.

In the Tudor age, the owner, William Hannam, whose initials are in the spandrels of a doorway, seems to have shifted the dais end of the hall from south to north in his revised layout of the house originally built by the Longe family. A fine oriel window in the solar overlooks the village street, while the south front overlooks a bowling-green. A decorative frieze of carved oak quatrefoils runs round the great hall, below a roof of the arch-brace collar-beam type.

Athelhampton Hall might be regarded, in one sense, as the swan-song of medieval manorial building in England, although it is nearly always described as a Tudor house. It lies to the north-east of Dorchester and is built partly of pale limestone and partly of the golden stone from Hamdon Hill in Somerset. The lords of the manor here were the Martyns, who had been the owners of this territory since the thirteenth century and whose tombs are in the church at Puddletown. Sir William Martyn, who built the house as Richard III was losing his crown at Bosworth, became Lord Mayor of London in 1493. According to legend, the palace of the Anglo-Saxon King of Wessex, Athelstan, stood here and gave the place its name, and it might seem that William Martyn was intent on imitating his predecessor on the site, for his battlemented house, with its heraldic glass and the chained

Athelhampton Hall, Dorset

The east front at Athelhampton, showing the private garden

ape of the family crest in stone ('He who looks at Martyn's ape, Martyn's ape shall look at him'), stands in ten acres of formal grounds with thatched stables and a contemporary dovecote.

The gardens were designed very much later, of course, but are very fine and worth visiting for their own sake. The heraldic ape in later versions has been given a Saxon crown and a mace but, in consequence of its humanized head, looks more like a chained slave. The spectacle here is the roof of the great hall, a marvellous piece of medieval carpentry with cusped braces. A Flemish tapestry on the wall shows Samson slaying the Philistines. An upper room called the King's Room is believed to be where the manorial courts were held.

It is possible that Thomas Hardy's master-mason father did restoration work at Athelhampton. Hardy's childhood was passed in the vicinity, and he knew Athelhampton well, the Wood family who owned it in his time having founded a Nonconformist school there. Hardy used Athelhampton as the setting for some of his poems and stories, although it was the lady of the manor of Kingston Maurward at that time, Julia Augusta Martin, to whom he was specially drawn, in spite of his mother having taken him away from the village school which Mrs Martin had started.

If Athelhampton represents the threshold of the Tudor mansion, it also represents a rough time for the rural population of England. The peasants might by now be nearly all free men, but their land was subject to enclosure and their labour to the whims of new landowners from the merchant classes exploiting the land for large profits. Sometimes arable land was destroyed by open-cast mining operations. Many new estate owners turned land into vast sheep farms to make their profits from wool. They needed less labour to run them, and they evicted their tenants and often depopulated whole villages, making peasants homeless and turning them often enough into town beggars. The feudal barons of old had depended on the peasants for their own livelihood – without men to work the land, they had no income. New economic forces dispensed with such reliance. Though feudalism had gone, the poor were often worse off than before.

Nor was the growth of the common law an unmitigated blessing for everyone. Under the manorial system, widows had been entitled to large parts, if not the whole of their husband's land-holdings. The amount varied according to local custom. But under common law, their entitlement was fixed at one third. This led to hardship among the poorer people and no doubt helped to swell the ranks of the witches in country villages who became the cause of such public hysteria in the sixteenth century.

An example of the sort of thing that was happening is to be found at Baggrave, not far from Leicester in an area peppered with lost medieval village sites, as if a shower of meteorites had bombarded the landscape. An eighteenth-century house, Baggrave Hall, stands in relative isolation now at the northern end of the former village where there were perhaps twenty houses in the fourteenth century. The lords of the manor were the abbots of Leicester Abbey, and in 1500 the land was enclosed, seven houses being either demolished or left empty when their families were evicted. After the Dissolution, the manor was bought by the Cave family. Thomas Cave was known as 'the Purchaser' because he acquired so much Church land when it was going cheap. Only two or three households were left there by that time. And time swept away the lord of the manor's house as well as those of his tenants. The moated site where it stood can still be traced.

The same thing happened at Ingarsby, where the Abbot of Leicester was also lord of the manor. It was a village of some size at Domesday, but by 1469 it was a ghost village, the landlord having turned the whole area over to sheep pasture. Today, one can walk over a hilly and bumpy field where the stone foundations of streets and village houses still lie under the soil where no human being has lived for 500 years.

Another case is Fawsley, in Northamptonshire, where Sir Richard Knightley acquired a manor which had grown in population from seventeen at the Domesday survey to about a hundred in 1415 when he bought it. But the new lord of the manor wanted the land for sheep, not human beings, and he gradually forced out the tenants by exercising feudal powers and raising rents to such levels that the villagers had to leave. By the Tudor age, 2,500 sheep grazed where the foundations of houses and the courses of village streets lay beneath the grass. A new manor house was built, later, to be landscaped with lakes across which the house faced the surviving village church where the Knightleys were buried through the centuries, but at last the old house came so far down in the world that it was used as a woodworking factory, with machines humming away in the great hall which had a fine open timber roof, a fireplace decorated with heraldic shields, and a superb large oriel window.

It is fair to record that the later Knightleys had rather more humanity than the ancestors who had set their family prosperity on course. It was Lady Knightley of Fawsley who courageously gave hospitality here to John Merrick, the Leicester man who was so hideously deformed that women fainted at the sight of him and who became known as the 'Elephant Man'.

Compton Wynyates, Warwickshire

CHAPTER 5

Tudor Expansiveness

The Tudor renaissance did not bring about sudden revolution-
ary changes in rural architecture or living-habits, any more than
the Anglo-Saxon invasion had done, but it did gradually free the
common Englishman from the stranglehold of a manorial system which had only slightly relaxed its grip in five or six hundred
years. By 1500, feudalism was, to all intents and purposes, a
thing of the past. New landowners were coming from the ranks
of those practising trade and law in the towns, like some of the
Pastons, and increasing enclosure was replacing the open fields
and commons. In particular, the enclosure of former arable land
for pasture, with the growth of demand for wool, was carried
out on an extensive scale, as we have seen, especially on
ecclesiastical manors, and the depopulation of many villages
resulted from this practice.

'For look in what parts of the realm', Sir Thomas More wrote,
'doth grow the finest, and therefore dearest wool, there noblemen and gentlemen; yea and certain abbots, holy men no doubt
. . . leave no ground for tillage, they enclose all into pastures:
they throw down houses: they pluck down towns, and leave
nothing standing, but only the church to be made a sheep-
house.'

'Assarting' – the recovery of land from forest or waste –
continued with the increasing demand for lands from a population rising again after the catastrophic plague epidemics, and the
drainage of marsh and fenland contributed to the usable land
area.

At the beginning of the Tudor period the mass of rural
Englishmen still lived in hovels – mud and timber 'cottages' of
one room with thatched roofs and bare earth floors; and all
cottagers, as Sir Francis Bacon said later, were 'housed beggars'.
They did not always take matters lying down. Simon Fish's
Supplication of the Beggars attacked the clergy as 'holy and idle
beggars and vagabonds' who had gotten into their hands more
than a third of the king's realm with their tithes and the 'good-

liest lordships, manors, lands and territories . . .'. The tract alleged that a woman who did not give every tenth egg to the church was liable to be declared a heretic, and that there was more profit for her in sleeping an hour with a friar, a monk or a priest for twenty pence than in doing a good day's work.

For the upper classes, however, some signs of change were on the way. Building skills were being transferred from churches to domestic buildings – particularly, of course, after the dissolution of the monasteries. Houses were better equipped with wall fireplaces, and Tudor manor houses sported many chimneys, often in decorative woodwork. Tableware of pewter or tin, or even silver, was replacing wooden spoons and platters. Although the great rebuilding of rural England was still a long way off at the beginning of the sixteenth century, the signs were already there, in a wealthy and powerful nation, that better housing for the common people would come at last.

Though the great hall, commonly referred to as a banqueting hall now, survived as a sort of communal centre of the manorial household, more rooms began to be created. Parlours, dining-rooms and bedchambers were supplemented by private rooms for guests and led to wings at both ends of the great hall, replacing the L- or T-plan medieval house with the pleasing symmetry of the H- or E-plan. The Elizabethans panelled their walls in wood and made sure that they had a minstrels' gallery as a sign of culture and refinement, though they did not immediately abandon the medieval gatehouse which perhaps was a sign of remembrance of things past.

The landed gentry took to hawking and hunting on lands which had formerly been reserved for the privilege of the king, though in spite of all their new-found refinements, their panelled halls were not always much improvement on those of their predecessors: 'All the rooms smell of dogs and hawks, and the walls bear arms, though it be but a musket and two corslets.' Alas, the English passion for dogs – already a talking-point on the Continent – has to this day prevented the nation from being as civilized as it likes to think itself.

In architecture, however, the need for symmetry became such an obsession in some quarters that it dictated changes in living conditions as well as absurdities in detail. Behind a window which was necessary for the sake of a symmetrical façade, a fireplace might be disguised; and because a newel staircase in a corner or turret was inconvenient for symmetry, 'grand staircases' were built in great halls, turning them into entrance halls instead of common rooms. Servants were thus relegated to the backs of houses with access by the newly invented 'back stairs'.

As Henry Tudor was claiming the crown at Bosworth Field, the lord of the manor of Calstock was building in Cornwall a fine new house of grey granite round a series of small courtyards. The Edgecumbe family had owned the manor since 1354, through marriage with Hilaria de Cotehele, and fragments of the earlier owner's sandstone house remain, but Cotehele is the herald of the Tudor manor house, even if its style is still largely medieval. The name means 'wood in the estuary', and the house is set in beautiful grounds overlooking the Tamar. Its preservation in such fine and authentic condition is due to the fact that the Edgecumbes, instead of changing the Tudor house out of all recognition in later times, built themselves a new house instead and left the old one alone, though continuing to take care of it. What is more, it became the first house to be acquired by the National Trust in lieu of death duties, in 1947, so this house built as Henry VII took the throne has been well looked after through five centuries.

Its great hall has a large fireplace and stone flag floor beneath a high, open timber roof, with armour and weapons hanging on the walls, and the solar has squints into both hall and chapel, which has carved Tudor roses in its roof and a clock, made in the year of Bosworth and still in the position where it was originally placed. The altar has a Flemish triptych of 1589 with the Adoration of the Magi on its central panel, and the other rooms of the house are hung with tapestries, some Flemish and others woven in Soho.

A small chapel on the cliff above the river is said to be a memorial built by the family after Richard Edgecumbe had escaped from Sir Henry Trenowth, a hit-man with a contract from Richard III, by leaping into the river, or at any rate fooling his enemy into thinking he had done so by throwing a stone and his cap into the water. It was he who built the house, but not before he had fought with Henry Tudor and helped to defeat the Plantagenet king against whom he had led local feeling. The Edgecumbes were duly rewarded with an earldom.

Somerset was a county which profited hugely from the demand for wool and the increase in pasture land, and it has some fine early Tudor manor houses to show for it. Croscombe Old Manor House is one of them, built by the Abbot of Glastonbury, John Selwood, with his initials held by carved angels on the stone ceiling of the hall oriel.

E plan at Barrington Court, Somerset

More outstanding as a whole, though, is Barrington Court, begun about 1515 and built in almost perfect symmetry on the E plan, long before Anne Boleyn's auburn-haired daughter, with whom that architectural idea is so often and so wrongly associated, was even born. Barrington was built by Henry Daubeny, Lord Bridgewater, using the mellow golden limestone from Hamdon Hill, and its architect gave it mullioned and transomed windows with moulded dripstones, gables with decorative finials, twisted chimneys and a four-storey gabled central porch, with a long gallery on the top floor such as Wolsey had at Hampton Court. The interior is of little consequence compared with the outside, for it shows a decisive if restrained move towards the Renaissance in style whilst remaining essentially Gothic in detail. The Phelips and Strode families followed the Daubenys here, but the house had become derelict by the end of the nineteenth century, and much restoration work has been done since it came into the ownership of the National Trust.

Even more spectacular from the outside is Brympton d'Evercy, on the outskirts of Yeovil, and also built of the warm-

Cotehele, Cornwall – the great hall

Brympton d'Evercy, the manor house in Somerset

coloured Ham Hill stone quarried not far away. There is a nice medieval story attached to this manor which, if it is not true, is certainly attractive. John Stourton, who purchased the manor from the descendants of the d'Evercys, had three daughters and owned three manors, and he gave this one to his daughter Joan as a wedding gift when she was married in 1434 to John Sydenham. The other two got the manors at Preston Plucknett and Pendomer, and we might be inclined to jump to the conclusion that Joan must have been his favourite daughter, but the present exquisite ensemble at Brympton did not exist then.

The Sydenhams became one of the largest landowning families in England, and it was in about 1520 that the present house was begun. Beside it is the older church of St Andrew, and between that and the manor house, a dower house built later for Joan Sydenham in her old age. The whole group presents a scene of unrivalled beauty from the west, notwithstanding its medieval lack of symmetry and indeed its somewhat hotchpotch construction, for the right-hand side of the front was built fifty years later than the left-hand side and in different style, whilst the porch was added in the eighteenth century using old stonework. None of this detracts from the comfortable unity of the whole ensemble, however, with its battlemented turrets, its mullions and transoms, and the curious bellcote like a lantern on the church roof. It is only when we see the south front that we lose the feeling of early Tudor serenity and intimacy. The building of this, at a cost of £16,000 late in the seventeenth century, bankrupted the Sydenhams. It is claimed that it was built to designs by Inigo Jones, but work was not started until a quarter of a century after his death, and it is clear that his spirit did not haunt the architect, for he would never have allowed one end of the façade to begin with a triangular pediment over the window and the other to end with a segmental one!

Midelney Manor, near Langport, and Bardon Manor, near Watchet, are much more modest, and both date mainly from the years of Henry VIII. Midelney was a manor of the Abbot of Muchelney until the Dissolution, when the manor house was damaged by fire and rebuilt by the Trevilians, who still own it. The brothers Richard and Thomas designed it as a sort of early semi-detached, having half each with their own front doors. The house was originally built of stone on the H plan, with gabled wings and mullioned windows. Parts have been demolished since, and the house has been largely remodelled, but one of its curiosities is the rare survival of a falcons' mews, built of brick in the eighteenth century, when hawks had already generally given way to horses in the housings which retained the name of the mews.

Bardon Manor is an unimposing house at the end of a lane in Washford, used as a craft centre, and might easily be dismissed as a not-very-old farmhouse until one enters it and finds a great hall which may date back to the fourteenth century. Sir John Leigh became lord of the manor in the sixteenth century, and he extended the house in which the 'Bardon Letters' were discovered in more recent times – part of the correspondence of Mary, Queen of Scots.

The manor house at Mells belonged to Glastonbury Abbey until the Dissolution, since when it has been the property of the Horner family. It was purchased from the Crown by Thomas Horner, not the *John* Horner who was mistakenly satirized in the verse which became a popular nursery rhyme:

Little Jack Horner sat in a corner
Eating his Christmas pie.
He put in his thumb and pulled out a plum
And said 'What a good boy am I.'

Nevertheless, the Horners acquired a stone-built manor house which is more famous for its literary and artistic associations than for its architecture, being rather plain and much restored. Thomas Hardy based 'Falls Park' in his stories *A Group of Noble Dames* on Mells, and his 'Squire Dornell' was the Horner who married Susannah Strangways of Melbury Sampford in Dorset.

The Horner chapel in the parish church has a tapestry in Pre-Raphaelite style by a later lady of the manor who numbered Edward Burne-Jones among her friends. Edward Horner was killed in action in 1917, and there is a monument to him by Sir Alfred Munnings, showing him on horseback, of course. Another Horner girl was married to Raymond Asquith, the Prime Minister's son, who also lost his life in the First World War.

Oxfordshire and Wiltshire may be represented in this early Tudor period by Compton Beauchamp and Brook House respectively, although it has to be said that the former is 'stone-faced' in its impudent occupation of a rustic seat in city clothing as it were, as well as in the sense Pevsner means, whilst the latter is incorporated in farm buildings. Still, they were born as Tudors, and Compton Beauchamp, standing in a dip below White Horse Hill, was born in Berkshire. It has a moat and was named after the Norman lord of the manor, William de Beauchamp, after whom it passed through the ownership of Fettiplaces, Holles and others before coming into the possession of the Richards. It was Edward Richards who turned the front into a stone-faced Palladian mansion, leaving the other sides in brick, and precious little is to be seen of Tudor work. Edward Richards' daughter Anne inherited the house when he died, and was much pursued by suitors who fancied her fortune as well as herself, but the lady's passion was for hare-coursing, and she died a spinster.

Brook House, oddly enough, also lies close to a white horse cut in the chalk hills above it, for this one is near Westbury, and although it has been much degraded since its days as the lord of the manor's home, it is of interest in connection with a disputed title to that office. The house was a two-storey building with stone buttresses, round-arched doorway and small two-light

windows, all looking positively medieval. The manor was owned by the Willoughby family at the advent of the Tudor period,
and Sir Robert was summoned to Parliament as Baron Willoughby de Broke in 1491, by a procedure long ago abandoned. The
title was not hereditary, and it fell into abeyance after the deaths
of Lord Willoughby and his only son. Nearly two hundred years
later, a male descendant through the female line claimed and
was granted the title and known as the *eleventh* Baron, the
previous eight having only been styled barons *de jure* and not
being peers summoned to Parliament.

Matters did not end there, however. The claim was contested
by Lord Brooke of Beauchamp's Court, who claimed that he was
also Baron Willoughby de Broke by virtue of the fact that a new
hereditary peerage had been created for his ancestor, a descendant of the first Baron through his daughter, who had married
Fulke Greville. This claim was allowed on the grounds that the
newly created peerage had extinguished the first, non-
hereditary one, which could not be passed down by females
who could not be summoned to Parliament. But in due course
the successors to the original title re-asserted themselves, and
the barony became a subsidiary title of the Earls of Warwick – an
odd decision, on the face of it, but then neither claimant had a
clear-cut entitlement to a peerage that was not hereditary in the
first place.

Snowshill, in the Gloucestershire Cotswolds, has a fine old
manor house built of limestone and now in the cosy company of
the village houses, though it was doubtless more isolated when
it was first built. The Abbot of Winchcombe was lord of the
manor, and his sheep grazed the hills all round the village, built
on sloping ground with its church on a green at the centre. The
house changed ownership several times after the Dissolution
and was much altered over the centuries, the hall being sub-
divided about 1600, a century after it was built. There is a
dovecote and a detached building which has a spiral staircase of
stone and which may have been occupied by the village priest in
early Tudor days. In more recent times, it was occupied by the
eccentric owner of the manor, Charles Paget Wade, who had
filled the main house with such a vast accumulation of cuckoo
clocks, penny-farthings and other irresistible trivia that there
was no room left in it for himself.

Sutton Place, beside the River Wey in Surrey, was built in the
1520s by Sir Richard Weston, whose initials appear with vain
frequency on its brick and terracotta ornament. Sir Richard was

King Henry's Under-Treasurer and went with him to the Field of the Cloth of Gold. He entertained the King at his new house in 1533 and gave the Princess Mary twelve pairs of shoes as a New Year present. His son Francis courted favour with Anne Boleyn and was one of those executed for treason, but Richard himself remained a favoured courtier. His house was originally built surrounding a courtyard, but the north wing with its four-storey gatehouse has since been demolished, so that one now approaches the symmetrical hall range across an open court, overlooked on three sides by tall mullioned and transomed windows and numerous terracotta cherubs over the doorway and in the parapets. The present great hall and long gallery have been altered since the house was built, but the hall's stained glass windows are original.

A later Sir Richard Weston was the author of a work on crop improvements and did much to develop better agricultural methods. He made one of England's first canals along a stretch of the river and irrigated his fields from it. More recently, Sutton Place was the home of J. Paul Getty, reputedly the world's wealthiest man, who was not inclined to follow the precedent of free hospitality to all comers set by medieval lords of manors, as he is said to have charged his guests for their telephone calls.

East Anglia was another area which throve on its agricultural importance to the great benefit of its manorial lords, and Giffords Hall in Suffolk and East Barsham Manor in Norfolk both date from the middle years of Henry VIII. The Giffords were lords of the manor in the late thirteenth century, but the Mannock family bought the property in 1428, and it was they who built the house on the site of their earlier house in about 1520. There are several memorials to the Mannocks in the church of St Mary at Stoke-by-Nayland, and the family remained here until 1787. Giffords Hall is a splendid sight, with its brick and flint gatehouse leading into a beautiful cosy courtyard and facing the hall with its porch of brick and timber, and with timber-framed ranges enclosing the yard all round. The hall has a double hammer-beam roof.

East Barsham Manor, which was built at about the same time, is an altogether different prospect. It is highly attractive, but in a more imposing way, with its stronger embattled façade of brick, and lavish decorative brickwork in chimneys, finials and mouldings. It was built by Sir Henry Fermor, and it is said that Henry VIII walked in his bare feet from a visit here to the Priory of Our

The gatehouse at East Barsham Manor, Norfolk

Lady of Walsingham, a distance of 2½ miles. He was a young man then, not yet embarked on his quarrel with the Church. Subsequent owners of this house have included Calthorpes and le Stranges, both of whose families had close connections with the Pastons; and the house was more recently occupied by a Hapsburg.

The name of Great Snoring seems more fitting for a rectory than for a manor house, and that is what the old hall now is, calling to mind such whimsically fictitious names for old manor houses as J. B. Priestley's Blessem Hall. But the brick manor house at Great Snoring was built seriously enough by Sir Ralph Shenton about 1525, with much ornamental brick and terracotta work, although Victorian 'restoration' did nothing to improve the place.

One of the most extraordinary survivals of Tudor manor house building projects is the famous Layer Marney Towers in Essex. Henry Marney attained wealth and power under Henry VII, rising further under Henry VIII, to become a Privy Councillor, Captain of the King's Bodyguard and ultimately Keeper of

Layer Marney Towers, Essex – the gatehouse

the Privy Seal, and he planned an ambitious mansion befitting his new status and dignity, in the manor which his family had held since the twelfth century. Lord Marney began with the gatehouse, commenced early in the 1520s and built of brick. There was no question of the building having a real defensive function, but its impressive design gives it the vague appearance of a formidable castle entrance. The three-storey wings flank soaring double turrets, on either side of the entrance gate, with seven or eight tiers of windows and much-decorated brickwork ending in ornamental battlements of terracotta, with fine twisted chimneys on the roof between them. The towers are square on the outside but polygonal on the side which would have been the mansion's courtyard. In 1523, however, Lord Marney died and two years later his only son and heir, John, followed him to the grave. The gatehouse had been completed but the mansion was never even begun. In different circumstances, it might have been just as well. Judging by the gatehouse, the Lord Privy Seal was out to rival Lord Chancellor Wolsey's Hampton Court Palace, in splendour if not in size. But with the Marney line dying out suddenly, and the local butcher's son falling from favour so soon afterwards, it hardly mattered, and the gatehouse remains as a strange reminder of a vast building project which was never realized, the bare rooms of the towers reinforcing the almost folly-like impression left by the barons whose elaborate tombs are in the parish church.

Gosfield Hall is a much remodelled house of about 1545 in the village near Halstead where Sir John Wentworth was lord of the manor. He built his brick house on a symmetrical plan, and his original façade remains on the west side, but so much rebuilding has been done by later owners that the interior has little to offer. In fact, the house has been converted into flats after being under threat of demolition.

The manor house at Tolleshunt d'Arcy declined in due course to a farmhouse but is an early Tudor manor surrounded by a moat and reached by a four-arched brick and stone bridge put up in 1585. The hall retains its original timber roof and doors from the screens passage to the service rooms, and other rooms have fine Jacobean panelling. There is a brick dovecote outside.

In Suffolk, Hengrave Hall was built in 1538 by one of the *nouveaux riches*, Thomas Kitson, a London merchant who bought the manor from the Duke of Buckingham. It, too, is moated. Kitson was Sheriff of London in 1533 and was duly knighted, so

Hengrave Hall, Suffolk – the west front

the house was an expression of his new standing in the world, and very fine it is, too. The building of the house is well documented. It cost Kitson £3,000, and we have the names of several craftsmen who worked on it – the masons John Eastawe and John Sparke, a carver named Davy, a joiner named Thomas Dyriche. It was John Sparke who built the bay window over the entrance doorway on the south side, a splendidly exuberant piece of stonework for which Davy no doubt did much of the preliminary carving. Hengrave is now a convent school, having retained its Catholic associations ever since Kitson built it, although one of his descendants only got a knighthood by promising Elizabeth that he would embrace the Church of England, which he did but briefly.

The oratory is one of the house's outstanding sights, lying behind the aforementioned bay window. It has a beautiful pre-Renaissance stained glass window, thought to have been made by the King's glazier Galyon Hone, in which scenes from Genesis and the life of Christ are represented.

Scrivelsby Manor in Lincolnshire was the ancestral home of

the Dymokes whose heads were Hereditary Grand Champions of England, whose sacred duty was to ride in full armour on a charger into Westminster Hall at the coronation of each sovereign, throw down a gauntlet and challenge anyone who denied the sovereign's right to the throne. This impressive tradition lasted from John of Gaunt's organization of the coronation of Richard II in 1377 until the equally inauspicious advent of George IV in 1821. The family arms included a crowned lion, and one stands over the gateway to the park where the old house stood, but alas, little remains of the Dymoke manor, the present house having been built after George IV's demise.

Irnham Hall is also only a shadow of its former self (though a pretty large shadow), having been gutted by fire in 1887 and mostly rebuilt after that date. But the original house was built by Sir Richard de Thimelby between 1510 and 1531, and some details of it remain, including a porch, some gables and the screens passage.

Across the country in Greater Manchester, Wythenshawe Hall survives from Henry VIII's time, though it has much Georgian addition. Surprisingly, perhaps, for that time, it has a symmetrical half-timbered front, with a central porch and projecting gabled wings. Diagonal timbers and latticed windows give us a hint of what is to come in the north-west of England, for though black-and-white building is called an unsophisticated taste, the Elizabethan lords of manors in these parts gloried in it and certainly left us some of the most spectacular houses in the country.

Gawsworth Old Hall, in Cheshire, has connections with a rather mysterious figure, for it was the seat of the Fittons, whose tombs are in the church and who are remembered in the inscription on the rectory doorway, standing near the church and manor house: 'Syr Edward Fyton, knight,' it reads, 'with my lady Mare ffyton hys wyffe.' The half-timbered house is not one of the spectacular ones, and in fact it was partly refaced with brick at the beginning of the eighteenth century. Indeed, before that happened, its then owners had already resorted to painting on the black and white effect. But its setting is to be envied, and it has a tilting-ground between its pools. What gives it special interest is its sometime resident Mary Fitton, who was a Maid of Honour in Queen Elizabeth's court, until disgraced through her affair with Pembroke, and who is widely believed to have been the 'dark lady' of Shakespeare's sonnets, on the very dubious grounds that the Mr W.H. of the publisher's dedication was

Gawsworth Hall, Cheshire

William Herbert, Earl of Pembroke, Shakespeare's young patron and seducer of his girl-friend. At any rate, Pembroke was ejected from court into the Fleet prison, for the Queen would not tolerate such conduct. After her death, he rose in prominence again. Gawsworth itself became a scene of scandal in the eighteenth century, long after the Fittons had departed, for there was a fierce dispute over the estate between the Duke of Hamilton and Lord Mohun, who fought a duel in London in 1712 and both lost their lives.

Shakespeare must have known Compton Wynates, called at his time 'Compton-in-the-Hole' because it stands in a hollow. It

Stepped gables and fancy chimneys at Chenies, Buckinghamshire

is not a dozen miles from Stratford and not far off the road to London. It was built by Sir William Compton early in the sixteenth century, with a courtyard and a surrounding moat, which has since been drained. Compton was a confidant of Anne Boleyn and helped to promote her romance with the King, not without self-interest, but he died of the sweating sickness before the romance reached its fruition. The arms of Henry VIII are over the doorway of his house, and one of the rooms is called Henry VIII's bedroom, but the great brick building, like Brympton d'Evercy, is delightfully irregular, without a hint of Tudor symmetry, unless it be in the topiary garden, and we see here that the medieval solar tower had not yet gone out of fashion. Some of the features of this fine house came from the ruined Fulbroke Castle, which the King gave to Sir William, whose descendants became earls of Northampton.

It was the earls of Bedford who owned the brick manor house at Chenies, in Buckinghamshire, and lived in it until they moved to Woburn. The earlier lords of the manor were the Cheyne family after whom the house is named. They were succeeded by the Sapcotes, and Anne Sapcote was married to Sir John Russell, but the new manor house was in progress then, if not already completed, on the site of the older property. 'The olde house at Cheyneis is so translatid by my Lorde Russel,' wrote Leland, 'that little or nothing of it yn a maner remaynith ontranslatid: and a great deale of the house is even newly set up made of brike and timber. . . .' Here, too, Henry VIII was entertained, but only parts of the large house he saw remain. Their attraction lies in the mellow old brickwork, the stepped gables and the massive chimney-breasts with their ornamental brick shafts – unmistakable signs of the Tudor quest for magnificence, which can be glimpsed in the Bedford Chapel of the church, a few yards away, where there is one of the most sumptuous collections of funeral monuments in the country.

We shall see shortly how the Russells rose from obscurity, but the Tudor monarchs were generally anxious to subdue over-mighty subjects, so that they were not politically dangerous. Private armies were rendered obsolete by efficient courts to maintain law and order, and by the appointment of Lords-Lieutenant who could call upon local militia when needed. Alongside the noblemen who were still socially the top dogs was the growing class of 'gentry' who became owners of manors, were eager to obtain coats of arms and called themselves 'esquires' – the name given in medieval times to those aspiring to become knights.

Hareston is a modest manor house in Devon built by John Wood around 1530 and having no pretensions to opulence, with a medieval plan of hall and porch and a wing containing a domestic chapel. The Wood family arms are over the entrance, as are the Fulford arms at Great Fulford, where the family had been lords of this and other local manors since the twelfth century. The date 1534 is in the hall, which has wood panelling and mullioned windows overlooking a courtyard.

Winterbourne Clenston Manor, on Dorset's chalk uplands, is more ambitious, though not large. Pevsner calls it 'compact'. It is also more characteristically Tudor, having been built to a symmetrical plan about 1530–40. There is a mixture of materials in this house – Ham stone dressings and mullions in walls of grey stone with horizontal bands of flint beneath a stone-tiled roof. The de Winterborne family built the original manor house here, which has now changed ownership by purchase since the thirteenth century, and indeed parts of the house date from earlier than the Tudor rebuilding. It has a stone newel staircase in the porch, and in the first-floor passage, a stone candle-holder in the wall.

Just north of Sherborne is that manor house which is Chingle Hall's chief rival for the dubious honour of being the most haunted house in England. As I do not see ghosts myself, I am not qualified to express an opinion on which house has the better title to the distinction. The stylish small gabled manor at Sandford Orcas was built in the time of Henry VIII, though by whom is not quite clear. The Knoyles were lords of the manor from 1533, one of them marrying a Martyn of Athelhampton, and the Martyn apes leer down on visitors from the gables of the house which stands in a walled garden. Servants in the house used to say that the apes laughed in the moonlight, and no doubt one could easily imagine other apparitions to bump up the numbers a little if necessary. Sandford Orcas acquired its reputation as the phantom capital of England after the burning down of the notorious Borley Rectory in 1939, and among its reputed ghosts are a tall fellow who was apt to rape the maids, a maniac who was buried in a secret chamber in the house, a farmer who hanged himself in the gatehouse, a priest who celebrated the Black Mass, and a man who smells of decaying flesh. You might think that this weird collection were all manifestations of one and the same person – a mad priest, perhaps, who turned to farming when he was defrocked for his misdemeanours – but of course that would seriously reduce the publicity value of the spectral platoon.

As for the house itself, it has a newel staircase at each end of the great hall, leading to the upper floor, and one of the hall windows contains original armorial glass. Its lovely warm stone from the Ham Hill quarries, and its compact design, mullioned windows and quiet country surroundings, make it a friendly looking place to anyone who is not half hypnotized before he gets there.

A manor house in Devon, Cadhay near Ottery St Mary, is often described as an Elizabethan house, but Henry VIII was still on the throne when it was built by a lawyer, John Haydon, who dealt in confiscated properties of the Church and used stone from the College of Priests in the village for his new home. The east side by which one approaches the house is symmetrical and was part of the original house enclosing a courtyard on three sides, the fourth side having been closed in by the south wing built later in the century with a long gallery, complete with curved ceiling – by that time very much in fashion, for it provided, among other things, a place for a beneficial promenade in inclement weather, with the family portraits to keep one company. The hall was divided horizontally to form two floors at a later date. I suppose the frequency of this operation came with the increasing use of the wall fireplace, when smoke did not have to rise of its own accord above the heads of the gathered company, and high roofs were suddenly seen as so much waste space. Parts of the original hammer-beam roof are still visible in the upstairs room. The Haydon who built the south wing also refaced the walls overlooking the courtyard with chequered flint and stone and installed statues of Henry VIII and his three children in elaborate aedicules over the doorways.

Ingatestone Hall in Essex was built by a Devon man, too – Sir William Petre, who was Henry's Secretary of State and also had cause to give thanks to the King, for the manor had belonged formerly to the nunnery at Barking. Sir William himself, like the vicar at Bray, accommodated his religion to the prevailing mood and thereby had a relatively smooth ride through the reigns of Henry, Edward VI and Mary, dying in 1572 and leaving the manor to his son John who became the first Lord Petre under Elizabeth. Their monuments are in the village church.

The great hall at Ingatestone has gone – demolished in the eighteenth century – but the house has a long gallery, a priest-hole, found beneath the floor in a small first-floor room, and stepped gables and original chimneys. This building was used as the model for the house in that bestselling Victorian novel *Lady Audley's Secret* by Mary Elizabeth Braddon.

Wharton Hall, near Kirkby Stephen in Cumbria, was built at about the same time by the first Lord Wharton from an earlier house whose hall remains, though much of the rest is in ruins, and the surviving building is a farmhouse. The hall was surprisingly large – on the same scale as the halls of Oakham Castle and Penshurst Place, though narrower – and next to it the equally impressive kitchen, over an undercroft. This was an ambitious building for the remote and poverty-stricken moorland of northern England, but Thomas Wharton belonged to an important family in the region. He founded the local grammar school, and his monument is in the church.

Farther south, near Preston, is Samlesbury Hall, which has also been reduced from its former glory but, unlike the rough stonework of the moorland house, is a picturesque black-and-white timber-framed house, built around the middle of the century by the Southworth family, who had already owned the manor for two hundred years. The great hall, a late example of the spere truss type, remains from the earlier house of the fifteenth century, and its high table was placed in a recess to protect the occupants from draughts, a perennial problem in the communal great hall which makes one wonder why the principle lasted so long. Part of the hall was demolished in 1835, and the movable screen was moved – to the opposite end where it was used to form a gallery. It was richly carved and bore Sir Thomas Southworth's initials and the date, 1545. Much of the later house was built of brick. Samlesbury is an exhibition centre today, and its grounds include an archery field.

At Hoghton, not far away, Thomas de Hoghton began the building of his impressive house in the 1560s, on land that his family had held since the fourteenth century, and probably on the site of an earlier fortified house. On its hilltop setting, a three-storey battlemented gatehouse leads to the first of two courtyards, and beyond it, oddly, is a garden in front of a range which once included the tower which gave the house its name – Hoghton Tower. It was destroyed in the Civil War, but the de Hoghton family still lives in the otherwise fully restored house which James I visited in Sir Richard de Hoghton's time and where the King is said to have been so impressed by a loin of beef served for dinner that he whimsically knighted it and gave us the word 'sirloin'. Swift gave his blessing to this tale, but it was the invention of a court jester, having also been told of Henry VIII and Charles II and arising from the mis-spelling of the French *surlogne* – above the loin.

Brick is the chief material of Plaish Hall in Shropshire, which is probably the county's earliest brick building, although it is very closely rivalled by the manor house at Upton Cressett. It was built by Sir William Leighton, an ancestor of the artist and President of the Royal Academy. He (Sir William) was Henry VIII's Chief Justice of Wales. The great hall had a hammer-beam roof, but this room has since been divided to form two floors. The upper rooms of the original house were reached by three newel staircases of stone. The appealing story here is that Sir William had determined to have the characteristic highly ornamented chimney-stacks of the period but was informed that the only local man capable of such craftsmanship as was required had just been condemned to death at the Assizes by none other than the Chief Justice himself. The judge promptly granted a stay of execution and, as we can see, got his chimneys.

*Decorative brick chimneys at
Plaish Hall, Shropshire*

*The courtyard entrance to
Wolfeton House, Dorset*

The Chief Justice lived till 1607. How long the felon lived is not recorded. One hopes he took an unconscionable time over the job! The house itself now seems doomed to dereliction, alas, its walls gripped by wistaria and its doors and windows half-hidden by invading vegetation so that it will soon look like the jungle-gripped ruins of Angkor Wat.

Upton Hall was begun around 1540, but a later date, 1580, also seems to be involved in part of the house, and it may be that only the gatehouse has legitimate claim to the earlier date. The main building was erected over an existing timber-framed construction and given star-shaped chimney-stacks as well as a much more unusual feature – windows of brick with mullions and transoms. The hall was subsequently divided horizontally to make a room above it, and this still has the timbers of the original hall roof. The house had been badly treated by vandals until the present owners took it over and restored it.

In Derbyshire, Hazlebadge Hall was built during Edward VI's short reign by a branch of the locally powerful Vernon family,

The former manor Hazlebadge Hall in Derbyshire

and a former manor house which has declined to farmhouse status sports the arms of Vernons and Swynnertons, with the date 1549, above five- and six-light mullioned windows in a gable whose old grey stone has now been rendered over. It stands at the roadside in Bradwell Dale behind a metal five-bar gate but is reputedly haunted by the ghost of Margaret Vernon, who is supposed to have died of a broken heart after seeing her lover marry another woman.

Henry VIII was yet alive when Wolveton or Wolfeton in Dorset was built – or at least part of it, for only a fragment of the house originally erected by Sir Thomas Trenchard in 1534 remains. Thomas Hardy described the place inaccurately as 'an ivied Manor House flanked by battlemented towers, more than usually distinguished by the size of its mullioned windows'. The only battlemented tower, in fact, is the stair turret at the corner of the great hall, and only this room and the gatehouse – which is actually flanked by unequal round towers in the French Gothic style – are of the Tudor period or earlier, the rest having been added or altered throughout the subsequent centuries. Nor is

Avebury Manor, Wiltshire

the ivy any longer there, having been stripped off to reveal the stonework. This house is well haunted, too, chiefly by the ghost of a later Lady Trenchard who committed suicide and was observed standing behind a chair at the dinner table with her head under her arm. The official account says her throat was cut, too, but this seems a superfluous detail in the circumstances.

The inside of the house, much of it Jacobean work, has some fine timber panelling and carving, and among many other motifs a chained ape, denoting a connection with the Martyns of Athelhampton not far away. What the significance of the parlour's plaster ceiling is, however, one hesitates to enquire, for the animals represented are unicorns, bulls, rams, stags, billy-goats and stallions.

Just preceding Elizabeth's arrival on the throne, but already having hints of the new look which was on the way with the great rebuilding of rural England, are Avebury Manor in Wiltshire and Sawston Hall in Cambridgeshire. Both of these houses, begun in Mary Tudor's time, were built from the start with a single-storey ground-floor hall with a great chamber above. Avebury was built on the site of a Benedictine priory or grange which had been granted to Sir William Sharington after the Dissolution, but the Dunch family built the house, Sharington having already been deprived of the property for appropriating proceeds of the Bristol Mint, of which he was Vice-Treasurer. Much addition has been carried out here over the centuries, and if the house pales in dramatic qualities beside the prehistoric stone circle whose circumference it clings to like a child to its mother's skirts, it is all the same an interesting and well-preserved manor house of the period.

Sawston Hall has sufficient drama of its own. The house that was here before it was built was burnt down by an angry mob in 1553, for Mary Tudor had spent the night in it as a guest of the Catholic Huddlestons, and some of the Duke of Northumberland's troops attacked it with the Cambridge rabble, in an attempt to arrest her and secure the throne for Lady Jane Grey. But Mary escaped in the disguise of a dairymaid, and when she saw the glow of the fire from afar, she said: 'Let it blaze. When I am queen, I will build Huddleston a better house.' She made John Huddleston a knight and gave him a position at court, as well as granting him permission to take stone from Cambridge Castle to build the house we see now. The stone is clunch, a hard variety of chalk, with some limestone and rubble. The place was nearly thirty years in the building, largely because of the constantly changing fortunes of the recusant family – there is a well-hidden priest-hole at the top of the newel staircase tower, designed by Nicholas Owen, who died under torture rather than reveal the locations of his ingenious hiding-places throughout the land.

The Huddlestons lived in this much gabled and chimneyed manor house until very recently, and the building has been changed relatively little since it was built. It has fine oak panelling, a long gallery and contemporary furniture and portraits which survive the army's take-over of the house for billeting troops during the Second World War.

Sutton Court at Stowey, Somerset, was built partly by the indefatigable Bess of Hardwick on the site of a medieval castle, fragments of which remain, including the fifteen-foot-high battlemented wall behind which the house hides. Mullioned and transomed windows grace a house which had been an asylum during Mary's reign of terror, founded by Bishop Hooper who was burned alive in ghastly fashion, in the name of God, after lying for months in the filth and stench of the Fleet prison.

A priest-hole at Sawston Hall, Cambridgeshire

Bess of Hardwick's part in the subsequent building was the north-east wing which included a parlour and private chapel, built in the year when Elizabeth succeeded her half-sister.

The philosopher John Locke was an occasional guest in this house in the following century, but by that time the preaching of toleration was not quite such a dangerous business. Bishop Latimer, who was consumed by flames in the same year as Hooper, had long been preaching against oppression at a time when the land question was one of major topicality. 'Lords of manors' could no longer claim customary tenants as part of their estates, but the most grasping ones enclosed common land, increased rents and generally exploited the poor, and there were peasant risings against these iniquities, supported by those who were trying to give the nation a much-needed social conscience, but not by the new Protestant landowners who held out nervously against Mary Tudor's popery, for they had frequently acquired their property from the dissolved monasteries. The legal rights of landowners were debated in an atmosphere of indignation and recrimination voiced by Robert Crowley:

Both for the housynge and the lande
That you have taken from the pore
Ye shall in hell dwell evermore.

But peasants who complained about the enclosure of common lands and the depopulation of villages were liable to be told, as one lord of the manor put it in a mind-boggling *non sequitur*: 'Do ye not know that the King's Grace hath put down all the houses of monks, friars and nuns? Therefore now is the time come that we gentlemen will pull down the houses of such poor knaves as ye be.'

But if we may return to Wolveton for a moment, the most significant story there, for our present purpose, is that of the enforced visit of the Archduke Philip of Austria and his wife in 1506, when a storm forced their vessel to put in at Weymouth. Sir Thomas Trenchard brought the couple here and, because of the language problem, sent for his young relative John Russell from Bridport, who was able to act as interpreter. Russell made a good impression on all concerned, and this episode marked the rise of the Russells to distinction and high office as earls and dukes of Bedford.

The special significance lies in the fact that those who rose to wealth and power under the Tudors were not the old feudal magnates but families rising from the new gentry because of their abilities in other fields than military service. They ascended through work, efficient administration, trade, the practice of law and so on, whilst the declining nobles sank ever further in wealth and power, neglecting their widely scattered estates through their desire for power without responsibility. The Tudor period formed a stratum of society which avoided the extremes that ultimately, and particularly just across the Channel, led to revolution.

Cothelstone Manor, also in Somerset, stands near the church in a delightful village of red sandstone at the edge of the Quantocks. Much alteration has been done here, particularly inside, but the gatehouse and front of the house look much as they did when built by the Stawell family probably in the first years of Elizabeth's reign, although the house is usually referred to as Jacobean. It is built round three sides of a courtyard and is more or less symmetrical, with shaped mullions in the seven-light ground-floor windows and attractive gabled dormers in the centre. The house was partly destroyed in the Civil War, for revenge on Sir John Stawell, who had raised an army for the

Cothelstone Manor, Somerset

King and been defeated and imprisoned. Tolerance had not extended *that* far, even by 1685, when the then Lord Stawell took Judge Jeffreys to task for his excesses and, by way of reply, saw two of Monmouth's followers hanged in front of his gatehouse.

East Lambrook calls little attention to itself, tucked away in quiet countryside near Martock, but the Old Manor there was rebuilt in 1584 from an earlier house, slight signs of which remain. The house is best known as the home of the gardening writer Margery Fish, who restored the old building which she and her husband found almost derelict in 1938.

The Midlands and East Anglia have a large crop of the best manor houses built in the earlier years of Elizabeth's reign. This is explainable, at least in part, by the appearance of the increasingly prosperous middle class of farmers, tradesmen and lawyers, some of whom aspired to become local squires and who built their new homes of the readily available limestone running through much of the region. The country in general saw a great proliferation of manor houses and a wondrous expansion of architectural ideas testifying to the new age of peace and prosperity among the landed gentry, if not through all classes of society, for it was only recently that Kett's local rebellion in East Anglia against the enclosure of common lands had resulted in the slaughter of twenty thousand sheep and the execution of the ringleaders.

The manor houses at Chavenage and Upper Slaughter, in Gloucestershire, built – needless to say – of Cotswold stone, are typical of a large number of modest Tudor manor houses in these parts, still wearing their warm coats of oolitic limestone and matching hats after more than four centuries in these stylish and well-cared-for villages, when elsewhere a great number of them would have fallen into ruin. The gabled house at Upper Slaughter is actually of Henry VIII's later years, or more precisely of Anne of Cleves's brief tenure of office. It did decline somewhat after the Slaughter lords of the manor upped and departed to America, but it was subsequently restored.

Chavenage House is of Elizabeth's time and was built by Edward Stephens, a sheep farmer whose family bought the manor of Horsley, in which it stands, when Mary came to the throne. Signs of an earlier house on the site include a stone spiral staircase, but the house is of E-plan design, though not symmetrical, the central porch having on its left two tall mullioned and transomed windows, possibly from the parish church, whilst the wall on the other side is relieved only by one or two odd bits of windows. Ghost stories have accumulated round this house where Cromwell and Ireton persuaded a reluctant Colonel Nathaniel Stephens to join them in the King's impeachment, and the turncoat, ignoring a warning that his own death would result from his involvement, followed the King to his grave within four months.

Harvington Hall and Grafton Manor, in Hereford & Worcester, both date from Queen Elizabeth's early years. Harvington was enlarged from a medieval house by one of the *nouveaux riches*, the lawyer Humphrey Pakington. The hall was on the upper floor of the older timber-framed part, the additions being built with red brick, also used to re-face the medieval building, which had a moat. The Elizabethan house is irregular in plan, and although it is not one of the most imposing of Tudor manor houses from the outside, it is a treasure house of Catholic manorial life, for its creaking floorboards and sloping passages harbour a fascinating collection of priest-holes and wall paintings.

There can be little doubt that some of the hiding-places were

*Harvington Hall, Hereford
& Worcester*

*St Thomas More in
stained glass at Harvington*

the work of Nicholas Owen. The most ingenious of them is in a small room on the second floor which has a brick fireplace in one corner, well blackened with soot, looking as if it had a fire in it regularly. This was one of the twenty-five fireplaces in the house assessed for Hearth Tax in 1666, for the family could hardly save themselves money by pointing out that this one was a fake. But no fire was ever lit in this hearth. The brickwork is supported only by the floorboards, and the chimney-breast terminates at the ceiling, for it is a hollow space providing an escape route to the attic. Another hole is secreted above the bread oven in the kitchen; another beneath the floor of a garderobe; and there are several others in this house of confusing passages, doorways and staircases where the third Humphrey Pakington was as much in danger as his resident priests and must have spent a great part of his life in constant fear of knocks at the door.

His daughter, Lady Mary Yate, spent her long widowhood here, dying in 1696 after being, as her monument records, 'Lady of this Manner 65 years'. Father John Wall was her friend and resident priest for a time, doubtless making use of the priest-holes when occasion demanded, before his capture and execution not far away.

Considerably more rare than Harvington's priest-holes, however, are its wall paintings. They appear mainly on the walls of passages and take the form of arabesques – decorative paintings done in black line and coloured with tempera. They represent human and fabulous figures and foliage and are probably by Flemish artists. The family had trading connections with Antwerp, and the brickwork of part of the house front is laid in the Flemish manner. The paintings are very much faded and in some cases almost indistinguishable now, but their survival at all is only due to the fact that they were covered with whitewash when fashions in interior decoration were changing, and soon afterwards the house was more or less abandoned for two centuries, being recovered from damp and neglect only from 1929 onwards, having undergone little change.

A curious and rather gruesome legend about Harvington, which stood derelict in the middle of a field for many years before being restored by its present owners, the Roman Catholic Archdiocese of Birmingham, concerns a family who were lords of the manor here after the Pakingtons. The Throckmorton family, who owned the house in the seventeenth century, kept a pack of savage dogs in a quarry cut out of the rock near the moat. A village lad had fallen in love with a daughter of the house and had to meet her secretly in the grounds, as her father would not hear of the match. One night, the lad, in making his way home, went too near the quarry and fell victim to the dogs, and in the morning nothing was left of him but his boots, with his feet still in them. The maiden went out of her mind, and her repentant father ordered the dogs (he would have called them hounds) to be hanged and thrown into the moat, which was afterwards known as 'Gallows Pool'.

Grafton Manor was also enlarged in brick and stone from an older house by Sir John Talbot, whose family had succeeded to what had been part of the royal manor of Bromsgrove after the Conquest. There is not a village here now, and if there was once, it must have been depopulated in the interests of sheep farming and capitalism. There is considerable cynicism, therefore, in the inscription above a parlour window, in a property of theTalbots, of all people:

> Plenti and grase
> Bi in this plase,
> Whyle everi man is plesed in his degre
> There is both pease and uniti.
> Salaman saith there is non accorde
> When everi man would be a lorde.

Contemporary with Grafton, but in complete contrast, is the half-timbered Mere Hall at Hanbury, built by the Bearcrofts who had held the manor since the fourteenth century. But Mere Hall seems to me like a bit of old-fashioned humbug compared with the restraint and good taste of the none the less spectacular Pitchford Hall in Shropshire. This superb timber-framed house was built on the E plan by a wool merchant, Adam Otley, and is surely the epitome of Elizabethan expansiveness in the Midlands. How accurately it can be described as a manor house is perhaps debatable, but that must apply to many later contenders for a place in this book, and Mr Otley certainly must have been regarded as the lord of the manor and addressed as 'Esquire'. The wool trade had been a great provider of wealth in Shropshire even in the days of the great Marcher lords. Besides, his descendant Sir Francis was Governor of Shewsbury during the Civil War. The only exterior concessions to flamboyance in this fairly large house were the diagonal struts in its timber-work and its many star-shaped chimney-stacks. The roof is of sandstone tiles from the old quarries at Hoar Edge, a few miles away, and

Pitchford Hall, Shropshire

the house stands in grounds with a lake and a charming half-timbered treehouse of the eighteenth century. The Otleys were succeeded here by the Jenkinsons whose heads became earls of Liverpool.

The name of Pitchford is owed to a spring which exuded a 'bituminous scum' identified as pitch in earlier days. The name 'Blackpits' still occurs on the Ordnance Survey map of the locality, and William Camden described how in Elizabethan times they ground and boiled a layer of blackish rock to make pitch and tar and distilled 'a kind of oil'. Could this be an island oilfield then? The fact of the matter is that Pitchford stands on coal measures with ancient rock fragments beneath, cemented together by sand and bitumen distilled naturally from the coal.

It is remarkable that in the same county, at almost the same time, the Corbets were building a manor house so utterly different in style as Moreton Corbet Castle. Sir Andrew Corbet's mansion was on the site of the family's former castle – hence the name, for the new house was in no sense a fortified building. It is in ruins now, like the thirteenth-century castle before it, having

The remains of Moreton Corbet Castle, Shropshire

Wilderhope Manor, Shropshire – stair turret and ornamental chimneys

been besieged by Cromwell's troops and burnt down afterwards. Even in its present sad state, however, it is easy to see that it was a remarkable house for the time. Built of stone, it consisted of two storeys with large mullioned and transomed windows, the upper storey being taller than the lower, with attached Ionic columns between the windows, all surmounted by a dormer floor with ogee-shaped gables. Its architecture was very advanced for 1579.

Shipton Hall and Wilderhope Manor, also in Shropshire, are worthy of mention, although they pale in comparison with both Pitchford's delightful magpie symmetry and Moreton Corbet's splendid design. Both are built of limestone from Wenlock Edge. Shipton Hall was built around 1587 by Richard Lutwyche, whose son John rebuilt the chancel of the village church soon afterwards. It was built on the H plan, but its great porch breaks the symmetry by being placed in the corner by one of the projecting wings. It is a four-storeyed tower, higher than the gables and soaring above the roof-line to rival the height of the brick chimney-stacks. There are stables and a dovecote.

Wilderhope Manor is of similar date and style and may have been erected by the same masons, for it lies nearby in a valley below Wenlock Edge. Francis Smallman was the owner of the house when new, and he opted for a single-storey hall which had his great chamber above it. Several rooms have decorated plaster ceilings, and the spiral staircase of timber survives in a house now serving as a Youth Hostel.

In Derbyshire, Somersal and Snitterton Halls provide a startling contrast in building dictated by the geology of their respective sites – Somersal being half-timbered and Snitterton of the Peak District's millstone grit. Somersal was built about 1564 by the Fitzherberts on a completely irregular and indeed somewhat eccentric-looking plan, with two overhanging gables to the right of the entrance making that part of the house appear distinctly top-heavy. Snitterton is more symmetrical, though not perfectly so, and looks a very restrained piece of stone building for its time. A stone rubble wall with a round-arched gateway leads into a homely front garden, and the house stands with gabled wings flanking its slightly battlemented centre range. It has mullioned and transomed windows, and Ionic columns (a later addition) at its off-centre doorway, but there is no Elizabethan exhibitionism here, and one gets for the first time a feeling of northern no-nonsense solidity.

The spirit of Elizabethan building is more characteristically

represented at Long Melford, Suffolk, where Kentwell Hall outside the village and Melford Hall inside it were both built at the beginning of the Queen's reign. Melford Hall may be slightly the earlier of the two. There is little of Elizabethan date inside the house, and indeed part of it was burnt down during the Second World War when troops were billeted there. The great hall has been polluted by eighteenth-century neo-classicism, and the long gallery has none of its original character. But the exterior, built round a courtyard and next to the village green, where a fine gateway leads to it, is impressive. Near the gateway on the green is a square brick conduit, apparently having something to do with the house's water supply at one time. The front of the house faces away from the green, overlooking lawns and gardens. It was built of brick by Sir William Cordell – another of those lawyers who rose to high office – on the site of an older hunting-lodge which belonged to the abbots of Bury St Edmunds. Stair and garderobe turrets are noticeable features of the house, two at the front and four at the back, all topped with ogee-shaped pinnacles. There is also at Melford a Tudor innovation – a gazebo or summer house. This one is built of brick and is octagonal, with eight gables surmounting chimney-like pinnacles.

The Cordells managed to steer a safe course through the religious rapids of the Tudor river, and Queen Elizabeth was entertained here on a lavish scale at the beginning of her progress through the county in 1578, Sir William setting such an example that Her Majesty's other Suffolk hosts were all broke by the time she departed.

Kentwell Hall is also, not surprisingly, built of brick and is surrounded by a wide moat. It is reached via a mile-long avenue of lime trees. This house, too, was partly destroyed by fire, but in the nineteenth century, and it had fallen into a bad state when its new owners began the job of restoration some years ago. It is a fine house of E-plan layout with a three-storey porch at the front and octagonal towers at the inner corners of its long cross-wings. This was the seat of the Cloptons, for there were at one time no less than six manors sharing Long Melford. The monuments of the Cloptons largely populate the fine wool church of the village.

It must have been one of these two houses which George Borrow refers to in *Lavengro* as 'the great house of Long Melford' where his tall girl-friend Isopel Berners was born and brought up. It was evidently in use as the workhouse then and had a chaplain who told the girl that she bore a noble name – very

The banqueting hall at Melford Hall, Suffolk

Elizabethan symmetry at Kentwell Hall, Suffolk

different from the gypsies, prize-fighters, horse-traders and eccentrics who made up most of Borrow's friends. Whether he really fought the Flaming Tinman and lived afterwards with Isopel is anybody's guess, but the reference to Long Melford's 'great house' is real enough, and Melford Hall is the likely candidate.

In Northamptonshire, we must return briefly to Sulgrave, where we first noticed the traces of a thane's hall, for a man of greater power than the Saxon warlord could ever have dreamed of had family connections with a later lord of the manor here, Lawrence Washington, a wool stapler who became Mayor of Northampton. The house he bought in 1540 was largely rebuilt in the Washingtons' time, though they sold it again in 1659, when John Washington emigrated to America and gave his new homeland a great-grandson of some significance. The stars and stripes of the American flag are commonly said to be derived from the bars and mullets of the family arms still to be seen in the spandrels of the doorway. The house itself is very plain indeed, but it is a shrine for American pilgrims seeking their nation's distant origins, though they are rather recent compared with those the Saxon hall-house represents.

Southwick Hall was built a little later on to a fourteenth-century house, part of which remains, in the huge royal hunting preserve of Rockingham Forest, where the King's court might order a starving peasant's hands to be cut off for poaching a rabbit whilst the presiding baron dined on venison. The present building is chiefly Elizabethan, with gables and transomed windows, but the medieval house was the seat of the Knyvets, who passed it through marriage to the Lynnes. They occupied it for a long period and carried out the Tudor rebuilding. The older parts of the house include a chapel with piscina, and the original newel staircase.

The country home of Prime Ministers – Chequers in the Buckinghamshire Chilterns – started life as the manor house of Elias de Scaccario in the twelfth century, but the present house of brick was mostly built in 1565 by William Hawtrey, a sheriff of Buckinghamshire and Member of Parliament, who had charge of Lady Mary Grey here when she was confined by order of the Queen for making something of a mockery of the royal household by marrying beneath her. The house is a completely irregular building of two storeys with many gables and multitudes of mullioned windows. Glass was now coming into its own, as glassmakers were at work in several parts of England supplying the goods which formerly only the very wealthy could afford to purchase from abroad.

Much reconstruction went on during the ownership of Lord Lee of Fareham, who presented the house to the nation (as it were) for the use of Prime Ministers, in 1917. Their reactions to the old place have been as varied as the people themselves, naturally. Bonar Law declined to use it, disliking the country almost as much as he disliked Lord Lee. Baldwin was happier as a country squire, and Ramsay MacDonald called Chequers 'this house of comforting and regenerating rest', whilst Attlee loved the area so much that he subsequently bought a house not far away. Churchill, characteristically, was unable to restrain himself from taking off into flights of rhetoric: 'What distinguished guests it has sheltered, what momentous meetings it has witnessed, what fateful decisions have been taken under its roof.'

Kelmscott Manor in Oxfordshire has sheltered some distinguished guests in its time, too. This house is of grey limestone and is surrounded by high stone walls and many trees in a quiet village at the edge of the Cotswolds. It was built around 1570, on an irregular plan with plenty of gables and mullions beneath its roof of stone tiles. Much addition and alteration was carried out in the following century, as was observed by a prospective buyer who came to look at it when it was offered for sale by a London estate agent in 1871. 'Elizabethan in appearance, but much later in date,' said William Morris, not least of whose achievements was founding the Society for the Protection of Historic Buildings. He nevertheless found it captivating and bought the house in partnership with his friend Dante Gabriel Rossetti, who was more interested in Jane Morris than in the house itself and would have lived anywhere she was. He soon became bored with Kelmscott, calling the village 'the doziest clump of old grey beehives' and soon leaving it, but Morris lived there for twenty-five years and called it 'heaven on earth'. He named his private press in London after the manor house and made it the terminus of the travellers' journey in his Utopian story *News from Nowhere*, illustrating the house on the frontispiece. When he died in London, he was brought back to the village in a farm cart for burial in the churchyard.

There are no legendary ghosts at Kelmscott, but it is not difficult to conjure up the spirits of such as Christina Rossetti, Burne-Jones, Ford Madox Brown, Yeats and others, all walking the grounds in animated conversation with Morris whilst Rossetti flirted with Jane Morris indoors, in breaks between painting her portrait.

Mapledurham House also has literary and flirting interests. The house stands in a remote hamlet by the Thames, below the Chiltern Hills, reached only by a narrow, winding lane. It was begun in 1581 by the Blount family whose descendants are still there today. It replaced an earlier timber-framed manor house, fragments of which remain nearby. A watermill in the grounds, said to be the oldest surviving mill on the Thames, may be contemporary with the house, which was built of red brick on an H plan beside the church of flint. A medieval lord of the manor, Sir Robert Bardolf, was buried in a new chapel built in the fourteenth century to house his tomb, and the Catholic Blounts retained the chapel as their private property, separating it from the rest of the church, although they subsequently built a private chapel in the house itself. A priest's hole in the house is said to lead by a secret passage to the church.

A great deal of alteration was carried out here in the eighteenth century and after, including the removal or adaptation of the great hall and long gallery, and changed to the symmetrical

Mapledurham House, Oxfordshire – central part of the west front

front with its gables, but much of Tudor interest remains, not least the oriel windows, fine plaster ceilings and an elegant well staircase.

The portraits in the house include those of Martha and Theresa Blount, and the sisters were the magnet that pulled Alexander Pope here, for he was no countryman, despite the love of gardens he had inherited from his father. The poet, deformed by curvature of the spine into a four-foot-six hunchback, fell in love with Theresa and Martha Blount in turn – 'two of the finest faces in the universe' – and left his property to Martha when he died, although his love had inevitably been somewhat one-sided. 'Blessed is the man,' Pope had written with characteristically caustic wit, 'who expects nothing; for he shall never be disappointed.'

Tales of a more gruesome nature are told of Fritwell Manor House, in Oxfordshire's stone country to the north. The two-storey house was built on the E plan towards the end of the sixteenth century and has frequently changed ownership – perhaps not surprisingly, for the story goes that two brothers named Longueville lived there early in the eighteenth century, and the older brother was imprisoned in an attic for fourteen years, dying at last of starvation and neglect. One version says that the brothers quarrelled over a woman; another that the elder brother was a lunatic. Perhaps both stories are true; perhaps neither. The attic has long since disappeared, and with it the cupboard called a 'kennel' in which the unfortunate man was alleged to have been kept. The house had undergone some alteration in the Jacobean period when it was owned by Edward York, whose initials occur in the drawing-room, and it was again much restored by the architect Edward Garner, who lived in it himself at the end of the nineteenth century.

A more authentic story concerns Sir Baldwin Wake, who bought the manor in 1730 and lived there with his two sons. During a game of cards one night, a quarrel arose and Sir Baldwin struck his eldest son in anger and accidentally killed him. He and his younger son hid the body temporarily, in their alarm, and the younger son disappeared in a successful attempt to take the blame on himself. The truth was only told by the baronet on his deathbed, his surviving son being then enlisted in an infantry regiment under an assumed name, and the title passed to the dead son's heir. There seems little doubt that embroidery of this true event, which must have prompted much local rumour and gossip, gave rise to the other story and became

confused about the period of its occurrence. Ghost stories naturally gathered about this old manor house whose real origins may
well be far back in time, for the village lies astride the prehistoric
earthwork known as Aves Ditch, or Wattle Bank, and pagan
associations enhance (if that is the right word) Fritwell's sinister
reputation. Moreover the church is dedicated to St Olave, which
suggests a Viking connection.

Ufton Court at Ufton Nervet in Berkshire was built around
1570–80, a timber-framed and brick house with a great row of
gables on its east front, though not symmetrical, and many
twisted chimneys. Its builder was the widow of Sir John Mer-
vyn, though there was an earlier house on the site, and she later
married Richard Perkins. She instituted the long tradition of an
annual dole to the village poor from one of the house's windows.
This was a Catholic house, however, with several ingenious
priest-holes, and in the time of the Perkins family the place was
notorious as 'a common receptacle for priestes, Jesuytes, Re-
cusantes and other such evill-disposed persons'. Searches revealed a chapel in the roof, 'full of Popische Trashe', but Francis
Perkins survived Elizabeth's Protestant zeal and died in his bed
in 1616. Arabella Fermor, the wife of a later Francis Perkins, was
the lady of the manor here in the early eighteenth century, and
this celebrated beauty was the 'Belinda' of Pope's *Rape of the Lock*,
having had a lock of her hair cut off by Lord Petre, resulting in an
estrangement between the two Catholic families which Pope
ridiculed in his mock-epic masterpiece.

The brick halls of Little Hadham and Little Gaddesden, at the
eastern and western extremities of Hertfordshire, date from
Elizabeth's middle years, Hadham having been built by the
Capels who became earls of Essex, and Gaddesden by the
Egertons who became earls and dukes of Bridgewater. Both
houses have been too much altered to proclaim their Tudor
origins too loudly, but Little Gaddesden retains a wall painting
which depicts the arrest of Princess Elizabeth at nearby
Ashridge, by order of Bloody Mary during Wyatt's rebellion.

The manor house at Chipperfield was built around 1590, a
modest brick and timber house with fine wrought-iron gates at
the front overlooking the village common. It has undergone
much alteration and became a block of flats in due course, but
the scene surrounding it has preserved its country character,
dangerously close to London, partly through the guardianship
of the Blackwell family who owned it at one time. Before that,
one lord of the manor of King's Langley who lived here was John

Parsley, a farm labourer who inherited the manor from his uncle early in the nineteenth century. He was middle-aged, illiterate and lived with his wife in one room, and with one old servant in the house. It is said that he abused his tenants with swearing and threats if they failed to pay their rents on time but would quietly drop a £5 note through the door if he knew they were unable to find the money.

The Tudor manor house at Garsington, at the edge of the Chiltern country near Oxford, had been a farmhouse for some time when it was acquired in 1915 by Philip Morrell and his wife Lady Ottoline. They spent nine years thoroughly restoring it and transforming the grounds into an Italian-style garden with ornamental sculpture and peacocks. In this gabled manor house of stone, which had been much altered in the seventeenth century, Ottoline Morrell gathered about her many writers, several of whom were First World War pacifists, and one or two of whom were her lovers. The house became a magnet for literary and political society, rivalling Kelmscott's earlier attraction for artists, though for a shorter period. Lytton Strachey, Aldous Huxley, Bertrand Russell, Herbert Asquith, D. H. Lawrence, Siegfried Sassoon, Rupert Brooke, Katherine Mansfield, Colette O'Neill and others filled the house, and whilst the lady of the manor entertained her more favoured guests in bed, the others overflowed into a nearby building which had once been the bailiff's house.

Mottistone Manor, on the Isle of Wight, was built in 1567 by Thomas Cheke, probably from an earlier house on the site. It is L-shaped, with mullioned windows, and stands near the church and the only prehistoric monolith on the island, a sandstone pillar known as the Long Stone. Sir John Cheke of this family was a classical scholar and tutor to Edward VI. His sister Mary had been married to William Cecil, Lord Burghley, but died within two years.

In the south-west, Trerice in Cornwall was built by the Arundells, of the local 'elvan' stone, a variety of granite which is difficult to work but which did not prevent the builder from adding some nice decorative details and is pleasing in its effect. The hall has a colossal window, for its time, on the left of the entrance porch – two storeys high and square with nearly six hundred panes of glass, which light up the minstrels' gallery inside. There are fine plaster ceilings in both the hall and the great chamber upstairs, and the original fireplaces remain, but the E-plan exterior is the eye-catcher here, with concave curves on the projecting gables and convex ones on the two which are set back.

In Devon, the manor house of the Tremaynes near Tavistock is Collacombe Barton, enlarged in 1574 from an earlier house, and most attractive with its elaborate stone gateway in the garden wall looking through to a simple granite house without too much ostentation, as is also the case with Dodington Hall at the foot of the Quantocks, built in 1581 and very well preserved, with a minstrels' gallery in its old hall which still has its fine roof of carved oak panels and its screen.

It is with the great surge of building activity in the later years of Elizabeth that the north of England catches up with the south, and where better to start than the spectacular Bramall Hall in Cheshire, completed around 1600 by Sir William and Dame Dorothy Davenport. The Norman baron who was granted the manor after the Conquest here was succeeded by the Bromhale family. It then passed to the Davenports by marriage, and this powerful local family who held many other manors in the county owned this one for five hundred years before disposing of the estate in the nineteenth century, and it now belongs to the Borough of Stockport together with the park in which it stands.

There is no simple plan here. Work carried out at various periods added to the south wing which remained of the earlier house, the great timber roof of the banqueting hall having been here at the beginning of the Davenport residence. Dame Dorothy is said to have spent thirty-six years working on the huge tapestry representing the Fall of Man, and there are medieval wall paintings in the south wing and a fine plaster ceiling in the drawing-room. By the Tudor age, wall paintings were to some extent replacing tapestries generally for interior decoration, as Falstaff indicates in Henry IV, Part II, when Mistress Quickly complains that if he does not pay his debt, she must pawn her plate and her tapestries: 'Glasses, glasses, is the only drinking: and for thy walls, – a pretty slight drollery, or the story of the Prodigal, or the German Hunting in water-work, is worth a thousand of these bed-hangings and these fly-bitten tapestries.'

Many of Bramall Halls's contents were dispersed when the property was sold, and it is the exterior that commands attention, in spite of the fact that much of it is a Victorian reconstruction. Damage was done here by both Cavaliers and Roundheads in the Civil War, when the then owner, also named William Davenport, complained of the 'rifling and pulling in peeces of

my house'. It had been built round a courtyard, but the whole west side was demolished in the nineteenth century and rebuilt mainly by the new owner, Charles Nevill. The place may not stand up to the close scrutiny of an architectural purist, but there is no denying the dazzling effect of this many-gabled magpie house, and it is typical enough in its sheer size and ambitiousness of the new ostentation of late Elizabethan – and early industrial – England.

Derbyshire lays unarguable claim to one of the greatest late Tudor houses of England, begun in 1590 by that builder of mansions and fortunes, Bess of Hardwick. But Hardwick Hall takes us across the dividing line between manor house and stately home, and it is the old hall to which we must confine ourselves. If ever a woman was to the manor born, it was Bess. Her father's manor was modest enough when his daughter Elizabeth was born in 1520, but although we do not know a great deal about him, the girl who was a widow at thirteen must have acquired her formidable, if not especially admirable characteristics from someone, presumably him. Her second husband was Sir William Cavendish, who was persuaded by his wife to leave Suffolk where he belonged and purchase the Chatsworth estate for £600, where the couple built a house and deposited six children. The mother of the Devonshire dynasty acquired the house, along with great wealth, when her second husband died in her thirty-eighth year. Never one to let the grass grow under her feet, she promptly acquired a third husband, also rich, whose wealth she steered to her own account before he made her thrice widowed within ten years.

Then she captured George Talbot, sixth Earl of Shrewsbury, ensuring her succession to his fortune before permitting his succession to her boudoir, but she separated from him fifteen years after their marriage, when she was sixty-three, no less, and set about rebuilding her father's old manor house at Hardwick, spending lavishly on its interior decoration and changing it from the modest building she had been born in to a huge country mansion. Hardwick Old Hall has long been in ruins, but it is undergoing repair in the ownership of the National Trust. It has some large multi-transomed windows, anticipating the famous façade of the new hall ('Hardwick Hall, more window than wall'), and inside some superb Elizabethan plaster friezes of forest scenes which Bess commissioned from the finest artists of the day.

Nine years after their separation her fourth husband died. The

Bramall Hall, Stockport, with instruments of justice

brassy Countess was in her seventies. She immediately began to build the new house known as Hardwick Hall, having her initials blazoned all round the parapets of its austere but ambitious exterior, so much like her own character. The old house was kept for servants and perhaps her important guests' retinues. The privy shafts in the old house were succeeded by close-stools in the new one, Bess having her private one 'covered with blue cloth stitched with white, with red and black silk fringe'. It was the only throne she sat upon, though her scheming imagination saw her grand-daughter on the throne of England, while she waited in vain for Queen Elizabeth to honour her with a visit. She must have forgotten the Tudor philosophy. Her estates were reckoned to be worth nearly a quarter of a million pounds a year when she died, a friendless old woman, ten years after she had moved in. She had outlived the Queen who was her only female superior in wealth and whose birth occurred when this other Bess was already a widow, experienced in life and death.

Staffordshire seems a little unlucky in its manor houses of the period. As if Ralph Sneyd's Keele Hall of 1580 had not enough to contend with in its name, inviting jibes about naval discipline, the place was rebuilt three hundred years later and then taken over in 1950 by the North Staffordshire University College, now Keele University.

And the Astons' timber-framed mansion of the same time has disappeared altogether, along with its successor on the site, leaving only the great sandstone gatehouse, recently restored, and the nineteenth-century stables as signs that it ever existed. The Catholic Astons had hardly completed their house when, in 1586, Sir Walter was given charge of Mary, Queen of Scots. She was in custody here for only two weeks.

Charles I created a later Sir Walter Baron Aston of Forfar for his services as ambassador to Spain, and the family were well-known patrons of the arts, Michael Drayton being among those who benefited from their favours:

> Trent by Tixall grac'd, the Astons' ancient seat,
> Which oft the Muse hath found her safe and sweet retreat.

Such virtues did not protect the Astons from Protestant wrath, however. The family steward, Stephen Dugdale, stole money from Lord Aston and made himself scarce, later accusing his former employer of implication in the conspiracies invented by

Titus Oates, and Lord Aston spent six years in the Tower of London.

The Tudor house was burnt down in the eighteenth century, when the title of Lord Aston was being used by members of the family with dubious claim to it, and the property passed by marriage to the Cliffords, who built a new house in 1780 which was subsequently sold to the Talbots. This in its turn was demolished in 1926.

The remaining three-storey gatehouse dates from 1570 and has been called 'the largest and grandest Tudor gatehouse in England'. It has turrets at the four corners with ogee cupolas, and a balustrade round the roof. Pairs of columns frame the large mullioned windows, Doric on the ground floor, Ionic above, and Corinthian at the top, and richly carved figures of soldiers and winged females adorn the spandrels of the archway.

The Norman de Mohun barons gave their name to a hamlet in Dorset called Hammoon, where the successor of their ancient manor is now an attractive farmhouse. It is of uncertain date but has a fine bell-gabled porch of Elizabeth's last years, probably later than the main part of the L-shaped house. Its roof is thatched, and it is built of pale Purbeck limestone behind a garden wall of mellow brick. It stands near the village church and is a splendid example of the small, friendly Dorset manor house upon which we could dwell endlessly were it not for the limitations of space in this book.

A modest manor house now in the suburbs of Birmingham was in the leafy lanes of Warwickshire when it was built, or at any rate extended, towards the end of Elizabeth's reign. Sheldon Hall was a brick house with stone dressings when it was altered around 1600 by the addition of gabled cross-wings with mullioned windows and brick chimney-stacks. Now it has been faced with roughcast and hardly looks imposing, and the interior, too, has been subjected to modernization, but it is interesting – and perhaps depressing – to imagine the lord of the manor surveying his green acres within a stone's throw of land now occupied by Birmingham Airport and the National Exhibition Centre, and itself covered with factories and tower blocks. The Sheldon family were among the richest commoners in the land once, one of their number becoming Archbishop of Canterbury and giving Oxford its Sheldonian Theatre.

Moseley Old Hall near Wolverhampton is but a shadow of its former self, its timber-framed structure having been cased in brick in Victorian times. In this case, however, it is the interior

The King's Bedroom at Moseley Old Hall, Staffordshire

which remains interesting, with its priest-hole and its well-authenticated connection with Charles II. The house was built by Henry Pitt in 1600 and passed by marriage to the Catholic Whitgreave family, and it was they who sheltered the King for two days after his defeat at the Battle of Worcester.

Another Catholic family built Benthall Hall in Shropshire, a brick and stone house with star-shaped chimney-stacks standing above the now-famous Ironbridge Gorge but built before industry had claimed the landscape, although the Benthalls themselves were early promoters of coal-mining in the east of the county. It, too, has its priest-hole, in a chamber over the porch, though if you believe the story that the stone discs in the porch walls represent the stigmata, it seems odd that the Benthalls should deny that there was a priest in the house whilst thus advertising their recusancy.

Hall i' t' Wood, at Tonge Moor, Bolton, was built in the last decades of Elizabethan England. It is a mainly timber-framed house with part in stone and is not large, but it revels in overhanging gables and ornamental timberwork, with cusped

Hall i' t' Wood, near Bolton, Greater Manchester

lozenges and St Andrew's crosses above curved braces. Samuel
Crompton spent his youth in this house and here invented his
spinning mule which was actually called the 'Hall i't' Wood
Wheel' at first. But the house was split up into tenements then,
and it has since been restored by Lord Leverhulme, with fine oak
panelling and furniture imported to represent a Jacobean yeoman's house, though one might think a somewhat affluent
yeoman.

Stonyhurst, in the valley of the Ribble, is now a famous
Catholic college, in a huge and austere late Elizabethan mansion
of stone, with extensive additions and alterations made through
the centuries since its commencement in 1592. Its great hall is
now the college refectory. But it began as a manor house on the
site of an earlier one which had been the seat of the Shireburns
since the fourteenth century. It was Sir Richard who started the
present building, but he died within two years, and the job was
carried on by his son. The fine original gatehouse remains with
its four-storey battlemented porch and twin cupolas added by
Sir Nicholas Shireburn early in the eighteenth century. By the
end of that century, however, the place had been abandoned to
dereliction, and it was then that it was offered to Jesuit refugees
from Europe who gave the building its new lease of life.

Gawthorpe is up on Lancashire's moors and is built square
and solid of stone, with rows of windows on three storeys so that
it might almost be mistaken for a small cotton-mill. It was built
between 1600 and 1605 for the Shuttleworth family who owned
it until quite recently, when it passed to the National Trust. At its
centre is a square tower, older than the rest of the building,
which is grouped so compactly round it that it looks higher than
its three storeys would suggest. The hall still has its screen and
gallery, and a fixed seat for the high table with a seven-light
window behind it, for this hall did not have a room at the back of
the dais end. There is a long gallery which has its original ceiling
and frieze and a huge overmantel made in the year of the
Queen's death.

She still had five years left when Speke Hall was built outside
Liverpool by the Catholic Norris family. It has hiding-places,
spy-holes and escape routes and is relatively unspoiled, but alas,
there is no escape from its surroundings – suburban Liverpool
and an airport runway – where once there were only green fields
and trees and a moat surrounding the house. The secluded
grounds of the hall itself are still pleasant, however. Various
dates are given to this superb black and white house, but much

of it was certainly built round a courtyard by Edward Norris while Queen Elizabeth was still alive. The great hall is an older survival, for it has a fireplace with William Norris's initials, making it 1568 at the latest, and the fireplace was itself a later addition to the original hall.

The richly decorated timber-work of the overhanging gables and all round the latticed windows are the chief attraction of this characteristic piece of north-western extravagance though; and it is not easy to believe, as you look at it, that the typical manor house hospitality had declined at this period, as one writer put it, to a 'troop of dishes led in by some black puddings, and in the rear some demolished pasties which are not yet fallen to the servingmen'.

Horden Hall and Gainford Hall, in Durham, are by contrast quite modest stone manor houses. Horden Hall, built by the Conyers family around 1600, is small and plain, with no other ornament than pairs of Tuscan columns flanking its doorway, but entirely symmetrical, even to a straight path from the central porch to the garden gate. Gainford is more interesting – tall and rugged with a gabled projection on each side of its square plan, and a long row of chimneys. There is a stone dovecote in the grounds of the house – now a farmhouse – built by John Cradock in the year of the Queen's death.

The manor house of Burton Constable, now in Humberside, was built in the Queen's last years, though its precise date is uncertain. Its restrained E-shape front of brick, though more or less symmetrical now, originally had its entrance to one side, into the screens passage of the great hall which has since been transformed into an entrance hall. The interior of the Constable mansion, however, is really an extravaganza of Jacobean and rococo design and includes rooms such as the Blue Drawing Room, Ballroom and Orangery, and the Chinese Room, all part of that multiplication of rooms and, while Elizabeth was still alive, an early sign of things to come.

One of the more impressive ruins of manor houses is at Thorpe Salvin in South Yorkshire. A small gatehouse with a stepped gable close to the village church leads one through to the perfectly symmetrical south wall of a house built in the 1570s by Henry Sandford. But this wall is all there is. It stands like a film set, almost uncanny in its complete façade, but with nothing behind it. Two round battlemented stone towers stand at the ends of the three-storey wall with central porch and, between the porch and each tower, a huge chimney-breast with four stacks intact on top. Many manor houses are reputed to have ghosts in them. This one is itself a ghost.

The Old Hall at Heath, near Wakefield, looks at first glance as if it might be a film set, too, standing at the edge of the village common and having the rugged northern look that one might expect in this industrial area. But this one is real enough, though small and neglected, and the lords of the manor, the Kaye family, were evidently intent on using their brass to stamp their authority on the village. Their arms are above the doorway, reached by one of those flights of steps which have the psychological trick of intimidating the visitor. The porch is in the centre of a symmetrical front with battlemented towers at the extremities and a highly ornamental balustrade between them. The other sides enclose a small courtyard, where there is a spiral staircase. The house dates from the end of the sixteenth century and deserves better care than it has received.

Oakwell Hall at Birstall was built by the autocratic Henry Batt in 1583. He misappropriated funds intended for building a school, sold one of the church bells as scrap metal and pulled down the vicarage. But the old manor house itself has a more enduring fame as the 'Fieldhead' of Charlotte Brontë's novel *Shirley*. As 'Currer Bell' described it: 'If Fieldhead had few other merits as a building, it might at least be termed picturesque: its irregular architecture, and the grey and mossy colouring communicated by time, gave it a just claim to this epithet. The old latticed windows, the stone porch, the walls, the roof, the chimney-stacks, were rich in crayon touches and sepia lights and shades. The trees behind were fine, bold, and spreading; the cedar on the lawn in front was grand, and the granite urns on the garden wall, the fretted arch of the gateway, were, for an artist, as the very desire of the eye.' The great hall is a fine panelled room with an impressive staircase and galleries on three sides. At the foot of the stairs is a pair of original dog-gates, to prevent the dogs in the hall from getting to the upper floor.

The only ornamental extravagance at Doddington Hall, near Lincoln, is the stone dressing of this long-fronted brick house built by Thomas Taylor in the 1590s. It is completely symmetrical and basically similar to Thorpe Salvin's remaining wall, with plain chimney-breasts between the projecting porch and the tower-like bays. It is restrained, not to say austere, with only domed cupolas to distinguish it from the plain brick Jacobean style we are fast approaching. Little inside remains as it was when first built, and the gardens are modern.

The dog-gates at Oakwell Hall,
West Yorkshire

Jacobean premonitions at
Doddington Hall, Lincolnshire

One of the more unlikely manor houses of the last days of Elizabeth I is Porters, now the Mayor's Parlour at Southend-on-Sea. This, too, is a symmetrical building of brick, with gabled cross-wings forming an H plan with the hall in the middle. Elizabethan panelling and fireplaces remain inside.

The south-east has several surviving but mostly much-altered manor houses of the period, Gravetye at West Hoathly being one of those which calls itself Manor with doubtful entitlement. It was built between 1598 and 1603 for Richard Infield, an industrialist who exploited the Sussex Weald's iron deposits before the revolution in iron-working took the profits elsewhere. He brought his bride Katharine Compton here, and their initials are carved above an entrance, whilst their portraits, carved in oak, grace the master bedroom. A more recent owner was the garden-designer William Robinson, who was responsible for the chief attraction of Gravetye today. The house is now a country house hotel. I remember the pronunciation of its name being argued between two parties once, one of whom maintained it was 'gravity' and the other claimed it was 'graffiti'. 'Grave tie' is its proper sound.

Grafted on to a late Elizabethan house, Plumpton Place is similarly a chiefly modern attraction now, Lutyens having worked on the place for the owner of *Country Life* magazine in the late twenties. Originally it was a timber-framed house with brick and flint parts and a moat, while Smallfield Place in Surrey was stone-built and uncommonly inelegant in this part of England.

Perhaps we may take our leave of Elizabethan England, in this context, at an appropriately ruined and characteristic manor in Devon. Berry Pomeroy Castle, near Totnes, was built by Sir Edward Seymour and his son on to the medieval castle remains of the de la Pomeroi lords of the manor. It passed to the Seymours by purchase in 1548, the castle having stood here since about 1300, amid thick woodland. One of Seymour's kinsmen was Henry VIII's brother-in-law through the King's third wife and, as Duke of Somerset, Protector of England in the reign of the young Edward VI, only to be executed for treason by Northumberland. Another kinsman had made more than the odd pass at Anne Boleyn's daughter in her youth and had also gone to the block, though not for that offence! Yet another Seymour, the Earl of Hertford, having been robbed of his intended bride, Lady Jane Grey, had married instead her sister Katherine and had fallen into disgrace.

Edward Seymour of Berry Pomeroy kept his distance from

Berry Pomeroy Castle, Devon

such dangerous involvements and built himself a large and expensive house around the courtyard of the old castle, with a symmetrical front of mullioned windows on three storeys, beginning at about the same time as the Duke was building his vast palace in London, Somerset House. The local lord's successor a century later welcomed William of Orange here. But the new place, like the old fortress, fell into disrepair, like so much that the Seymours were involved in, having suffered much damage in the Civil War and in a fire in 1708. It stands like a symbol of the Tudor demise, built proudly on medieval foundations and representing England's new-found power and greatness, but soon to be superseded by new ideas.

CHAPTER 6

The Country Squire's House

The Stuart century began by continuing the great rebuilding of rural England and bringing in the age of secular architecture, and ended with the transformation of the baronial overlords' despotism of former times into the patriarchy of the country squires. John Aubrey was among those who had reservations about the rising class of landowners who had no links with the hereditary nobility: '. . . by selling of the church-lands, is the ballance of the Government quite altered, and put in the hands of the Common people.' The landed gentry and the wealthy tradesmen who set themselves up as latterday lords of the manor received not a little abuse from the more conservative observers of society and its changes: 'His father was a man of good stocke,' wrote John Earle in 1628, 'though but a Tanner, or Usurer; hee purchast the Land, and his son the Title.'

Purchasing titles was not within the means of all those who might have liked the idea, however, nor was pretension to refinement, for, as Macauley says, if the heir of an estate went to school and college, 'he generally returned before he was twenty to the seclusion of the old hall, and there, unless his mind were very happily constituted by nature, soon forgot his academical pursuits in rural business and pleasures. His chief serious employment was the care of his property.'

Nevertheless, the image Macaulay paints of the typical English country squire of James II's time – an unlettered local magistrate, swilling ale when he was not out hunting, freely cursing Frenchmen and Scotchmen as well as Quakers and Jews, cultivating his farmland's soil but not his children's brains, handling pigs on market days and growing cabbages close to his hall door, is perhaps more picturesque than accurate, for there was, as we shall see, a growing sense of taste and discrimination among the landed gentry, reflected above all in the style and comfort of their houses and in the contempt which some of them now felt for the country life. 'I have not yet been a day in the country,' wrote Lord Pembroke at Wilton in 1601, 'and

Gunby Hall, Lincolnshire

I am as weary of it as if I had been a prisoner there seven year.'

Until the Civil War, life under the Stuarts was much the same for rural Englishmen as under Elizabeth. It was a period of consolidation, and the new adventurousness abroad and the growing importance of the towns at home had little apparent connection with the yeoman farmer or husbandman. The village farmers were now living in relatively decent and solidly built cottages of timber, brick or even stone, of a type that the lord of the manor himself might have occupied a couple of centuries earlier, but the poorer labourers still lived in two-room huts made of mud and clay, or even turf, with bare earth floors and their fire still in the centre, their few pigs and poultry sharing the thatched roof over their heads. The great rebuilding had not yet extended that far down the social scale.

There was, on the other hand, increasing debate about the land question and the condition of the poor, and although enclosure was now an unstoppable force, some checks were made against indiscriminate enclosure by unscrupulous land-owners, in response to a century of opposition from such powerful preachers as Latimer and Laud. For as Gerard Win-stanley, leader of the short-lived community of 'Diggers' during the Commonwealth said: '. . . seeing the common people of England, by joynt consent of person and purse, have cast out Charles . . . the land now is to returne into the joynt hands of . . . the commonours', for the victory over the oppressors repre-sented by the King would not be complete as long as the people 'remayne slaves still to the kingly power in the hands of lords of manors'.

The 'lords of manors' were thus under increasing moral and economic pressure, and the landed gentry was in a greater state of flux than ever before. Many wealthy families disappeared, through failure of the male line in times of high infant mortality; many others declined to yeoman status, through mismanage-ment leading to the selling of their estates, if not actual bank-ruptcy; and new men rose to take their places having made money at trade or the practice of law or the careful building up of capital from agriculture.

The main change in the style of the house which the 'lord of the manor' lived in, apart from its external architecture, was the multiplicity of rooms. The taste for privacy, which had once been the privilege of the nobility, had begun to spread in the late Tudor period to all classes of society, and the Stuart period saw the slow decline of the great hall of two-storey height, in favour of a less communal way of life in which a larger number of rooms was favoured, smaller than hitherto but each having its own special purpose. And one of the purposes might well be a library. Macauley's ignorant squire might be in the majority, but there were many country gentlemen who read books regularly, absorbing the ideas of thinkers on religion, history and politics which the printing press was now making universally available.

The Jacobean manor house also dispensed with the central courtyard, and the tapestries and wall paintings which had for so long decorated the rooms gave way more and more to timber panelling and to framed pictures, while the floors were carpeted and the gardens outside stocked with flowers and fruit trees in a new passion which has not wavered since.

Bramshill House, near Hampshire's border with Berkshire, is the early Jacobean country house *par excellence*. It was built on the site of an earlier house by Lord Zouche in 1605–12 and at the end of the century became the seat of the baronets of the Cope family. The house has three storeys and is built of brick, with a highly ornamental central range and projecting wings surmounted by a decorative parapet. It still has a courtyard and a great hall, but there its connection with medievalism ends, for open staircases lead to the upper floors, and above the hall is a drawing-room, while marble chimney-pieces are the focal points of several rooms both upstairs and down. More significantly still, the house is set in its own parkland.

Bramshill was for long associated with the legend of the 'Mistletoe Bough' – without any more evidence than in the case of Minster Lovell Hall, which is still mentioned in connection with the legend in guidebooks. No one knows the origin of this story of a young bride who, playing a game of hide-and-seek at Christmas, accidentally locked herself in an oak chest and was never found until her skeleton was discovered generations afterwards. A more securely based tale of Bramshill is that an Archbishop of Canterbury was a member of a shooting party on Lord Zouche's estate here in 1621, and he accidentally shot a keeper. He observed a weekly fast-day for the rest of his life and settled an annuity of £20 on the poor widow, but the incident did little for his image with the lower clergy and reminds me of a remark of the Rev. Sydney Smith: 'If anything ever endangers the Church, it will be the strong propensity to shooting for which the clergy are remarkable. Ten thousand good shots dispersed over the country do more harm to the cause of religion than the arguments of Voltaire and Rousseau.'

The Archbishop was an unlucky member of the battalions of clergymen who have for centuries joined the village squires in the 'sport' of hunting which led Matthew Arnold to call the stately homes of England, with some justice, 'outposts of barbarism'. To this day the 'gentlemen' who enjoy hunting seem to believe that they are entitled to behave like feudal lords of the manor. In the very week I write these lines I have heard of a lady, who complained to a Master of Foxhounds about damage done to her garden by his dogs, being told to shut her mouth.

Arreton Manor, on the Isle of Wight, was built around 1639 for Sir Humphrey Bennet, but as the monuments in the village church show, it was the Holmes family that rose to greatest prominence here in the eighteenth century. It is a small stone house of H plan, with mullioned windows and panelled rooms, and it replaced an earlier manor on the site which was in royal hands at the time of the Conquest, then passed to Quarr Abbey until the Dissolution, when Henry VIII possessed it again for the Crown until Charles I disposed of it to help pay his debts.

At the other end of the country, Meaburn Hall at Maulds Meaburn, built at the same time as Bramshill, perhaps indicates more than anything else, in its similar style and stateliness, the improvement in communications which was helping this part of the country to become less isolated and backward, though Lord Lonsdale's storing in a cupboard of his second wife's embalmed body, in a coffin with a glass lid, might suggest otherwise.

Welton Hall, across the Pennines, seems to have been built about the same time on to a defensive medieval tower which had itself been built of material from the Roman wall near which it stands. The L-shaped manor house has mullioned windows, like most stone houses of the period, but this house is now part of a farm complex, and the tower is in ruins. The pele tower was in any case by this time giving way to the more conventional manor house in the relatively peaceful far north of England.

Washington Old Hall, now in Tyne & Wear, is well known as the ancestral home of the Washington family who gave the United States their first President, they having been here since the twelfth century, but the present house, restored with American financial aid, is characteristic early Jacobean, though built of stone on a small scale, with hall, kitchen and drawing-room on the ground floor, and the inevitable mullioned windows.

One of the most spectacular façades of the Jacobean period is Howsham Hall in South Yorkshire. The interior of this house, which eventually became a prep school, was much altered late in

Robust northern stonework at Washington Old Hall, Tyne & Wear

the eighteenth century, but the south front of grey limestone, of about 1619, remains perfect: symmetrical with multitudinous windows, mullioned and transomed, on two storeys capped by a series of semicircular mini-gables with ball finials on top.

Formerly in West Yorkshire but now in Lancashire is Browsholme Hall, near Clitheroe. The house is built of red sandstone, has a symmetrical façade with projecting wings and is notable for the fine woodwork in the Oak Parlour, and the museum-like collection of antiquities belonging to the family who built the house and still occupy it, the Parkers. One of these curiosities is a 'dog-gauge', dating from the time when no one but the lord of the manor was allowed to keep dogs large enough to be used for hunting. If a dog's head would not pass through the metal ring, it was illegal.

Also in Lancashire, Astley Hall at Chorley has building of various times but was chiefly erected during the reign of Charles I and in the Commonwealth period, for the Charnock family who had held the manor since the fifteenth century. It has a square and solid northern look about it but is saved from over-heaviness by the extraordinary profusion of glass in the main façade. When the windows are seen reflected in the lake, the scene is picturesque in spite of the house's squareness, its clumsy details and its lack of symmetry due to its having been built on to an earlier timber-framed house. But two bay windows rise to the full height of the house, with a balustrade along the roof line, and the upper windows in these continue an unbroken row of mullioned and transomed windows which light the whole length of the long gallery. Unfortunately, cement rendering covers the Jacobean brickwork and adds to the somewhat down-market look of the place, which is emphasized inside by the spectacular but tasteless plaster ceilings of hall, morning room and drawing-room and the excessively carved Jacobean staircase, to say nothing of the panels in the hall with paintings of such an extraordinary and inexplicable collection of figures as Tamerlane, Columbus, Queen Elizabeth I, Mohammed II, Spinola and William of Orange, among others. The MP Thomas Charnock, whose son was the last of the line, was responsible for these being here, and one wonders how his mind worked to conceive such an ill-assorted gallery of rogues and heroes.

In Norfolk, Barningham Hall was built in 1612 for Sir Edmund Paston, a name still to be reckoned with in these parts, and his house shows a fine Jacobean front of red brick, with oddly

Quenby Hall, Leicestershire

double-storeyed dormers. The house stands in its own park with the partly ruined church.

Quenby Hall in Leicestershire is a symmetrical brick-built house of about 1615–20 built for George Ashby, who was enough of a traditionalist to retain a great hall with screens passage, though the house has a Grand Staircase, a library, a dining-room, panelled bedrooms and a parlour above the hall. His family were sufficiently traditionalist, also, to destroy the village which once stood here in order to create their large park. The house stands on high ground with its mullioned windows overlooking the undulating shires country around it where the Quorn Hunt chases the fox, and there are some grounds for believing the house – or at any rate the kitchen – to be the birthplace of Stilton, that king of cheeses being often credited to Elizabeth Scarbrow, who was housekeeper at Quenby Hall until she became Mrs Orton and moved to Little Dalby. The servants' quarters were in one wing of the house well apart from the family's private rooms in the other.

Woolsthorpe Manor in Lincolnshire has a dubious connection

with fallen apples, this being the birthplace of Isaac Newton, whose mother, Hanna, said her baby was so small she could have cradled him in a quart mug. Woolsthorpe, built about 1620, is of no great size itself, but it produced great things when it sheltered Newton during the plague in 1666, when many of the young mathematician's ideas took form.

Hainton Hall is the ancestral home of the family whose tombs dominate the parish church, the Heneages. Probably completed in 1638, the house has since been much altered, as has Harrington Hall not far away, where the Copledykes held the medieval manor for centuries. The name is variously spelt in the church monuments – Copuldyk, Copeldyckx, Copledike – but by the time the new house was built, they had gone, and Vincent Ancotts was here, retaining the Tudor porch of a house that he entirely remodelled in the new style around 1673.

In 1661, Clement Paston wrote to his brother John that 'Wyndham is come to town . . . and he saith that he will have Felbrigg again ere Michaelmas, or there shall be 500 heads broke therefore.' And sure enough, the Wyndhams succeeded to the estate long held by the Felbriggs whose memorials are in the church alongside those of their successors. The church stands in the park with the hall, the former village here having disappeared like that at Quenby, and doubtless for the same reason. It was Thomas Windham who built the present house around 1620, in characteristic Jacobean style in brick, with mullioned windows below a stone parapet with the words 'Gloria Deo In Excelsis' carved out, and three sets of triple star-shaped chimney-stacks. Inside, the hall is supplemented by drawing-room and library among other rooms, and of course the fashionable Grand Staircase. In the grounds is a rebuilt stable block and a brick dovecote. The Windhams or Wyndhams of Norfolk were related to those who became earls of Egremont and built Petworth House in Sussex later in the century – a stately home on the site of their former manor house.

The manor of Blickling was purchased in 1616 by Sir Henry Hobart, Lord Chief Justice and one of James I's new baronets, who began the building of Blickling Hall – completed in the next dozen or so years – on the site of a previous manor house which had at one time belonged to Sir John Fastolf and then to Anne Boleyn's great-grandfather. It is one of the finest Jacobean houses in England, built on such a scale that it might, like Petworth, be regarded as a palace, but it qualifies for inclusion here, like Haddon Hall, by virtue of its origin and history. In the

The ceiling of the long gallery at Blickling Hall, Norfolk

grounds are several items which were brought here from the Pastons' manor at Oxnead, where the heads of the family had become earls of Yarmouth and had bought statues from the sculptor Nicholas Stone, before their fortunes declined and Oxnead was sold and demolished.

The house was in all probability the work of Robert Lyminge. Dining-room, drawing-rooms, ante-rooms and bedrooms all give way in splendour here to the long gallery, nearly 130 feet in length, with its superb library and a sumptuous moulded plaster ceiling which typifies more than anything else of this period the taste for architectural luxury which was now within the expectations of aspiring lords of manors.

Dorset is particularly well endowed with manor houses of the seventeenth century up to and including the Civil War and Commonwealth, and it will be interesting to take them all together. Among the earlier ones is Poxwell Manor, not far from Weymouth and built of Purbeck limestone. Pevsner says that 'what strikes one altogether about Poxwell is its limpness as a design.' Well, that is if one is looking for architectural ambitiousness or audacity. What strikes me about Poxwell is its simplicity and homeliness, an encouraging sign in a class temperamentally inclined towards megalomania. Its funny little octagonal gazebo or gatehouse with conical roof gives it just a modest touch of the picturesque in front of its mullioned and transomed windows. It was built for the merchant John Henning, and I should think he was happy enough in it, which is more important than what posterity might think of his architect. Hardy gave it the name of Oxwell in *The Trumpet Major* and domiciled Squire Derriman there.

Anderson Manor, further north, is more formal and conventional for its time – a symmetrical brick E-plan façade with stone dressings and tall chimneys, though the other sides of the house are fairly nondescript, and indeed there is even cement rendering on some walls. This house was built for John Tregonwell III of Milton Abbas in 1622, and every third course of fired pink bricks was burnt in dark purple, giving the house its general plum colour with grey dressings of Purbeck limestone.

Waterston Manor, near Puddletown, post-dates Anderson by perhaps twenty years. The old house on the site had belonged to the Martyns before they moved to Athelhampton. Set back from the road through a wide-arched gatehouse covered in wistaria and surmounted by a weathervane, the modern house is built chiefly in brick, though partly rendered and with some stone. As

Woolbridge Manor, Dorset

if this were not enough of a jumble, a classical façade on an east gable, dated 1586 and evidently acquired from another property, minus the statues which once stood in its lower niches, makes this an uncharacteristically bitty kind of house, and it is no great surprise to learn that it was in use as a farmhouse in Hardy's youth, before a fire in 1863 did much damage and eventually led to its restoration. Hardy made it the home of Bathsheba Everdene in *Far from the Madding Crowd*. Manor houses had a compelling fascination for Hardy.

Woolbridge Manor, now an hotel, also has close associations with him. Standing beside the River Frome across a five-arched bridge, it looks particularly attractive in its open farmland setting. The house was originally built in the Elizabethan period but was largely rebuilt in the seventeenth century, probably both before and after the Civil War. It was once the home of the Turberville family, and here Hardy set the tragic honeymoon of Tess of the d'Urbervilles and Angel Clare, where Tess going upstairs was alarmed by the life-size portraits in profile of two ugly women on the wall – 'ladies of the d'Urberville family', as she was told, 'the ancient lords of this manor'. The years have worn the heads away now, but the imagination can still picture the unhappy young couple whose past caught up with them in this old place.

Cranborne Manor is altogether more pure and splendid and brings us to the Civil War period, for the Cecil family acquired the manor early in the century and carried out alterations to the medieval hunting-lodge right up to 1647, after which it was little altered for more than two centuries. The great Robert Cecil, son of Lord Burghley and first Earl of Salisbury, entertained James I here, having turned the battlemented lodge into an almost accidentally beautiful house with tall brick chimney-stacks above high latticed windows and an Italian-style loggia, all behind a garden wall of random rubble and a gateway flanked by trees.

The next earl entertained Charles I here, and during the Civil War, Cranborne was sacked, not by the Parliamentarians, as might be expected, but by the Royalists, for Salisbury had changed sides in the meantime. Prince Rupert's men killed an ox in the Great Hall and left the place looking, according to Lord Salisbury's bailiff, 'as nasty as a butcher's yard'. Traces of the medieval house survive. It was built above an undercroft and had a private chapel and a garderobe projection. Robert Cecil acquired the hunting rights of Cranborne Chase with the semi-derelict house, and his reconstructions began in 1608, adding new wings, which have since disappeared, to make a symmetrical front. It was in 1647 when the west wing was built by his successor, with a hipped roof that caused some argument at the time. The interior house has been modernized.

In Somerset, Hinton House at the lovely village of Hinton St George was the seat of the Poulett family until its sale in recent years, and the village church is crowded with their monuments. Sir Amyas Poulett was the guardian of Mary, Queen of Scots, for a time at Fotheringhay, and Queen Elizabeth suggested to him that he should quietly murder his charge, mocking his refusal on grounds of conscience as 'daintiness'. His father, Sir Hugh, apparently built the original house here, but the present building dates from the first Baron Poulett's time, replacing the 'goodly Manor Place' referred to by Leland but regarded by Sir James Poulett as a 'dull, dirty place'.

The Civil War interrupted, and indeed ended, the building of Godolphin House in Cornwall, where the local lords of the manor made their fortunes out of the tin mines whose derelict

The classical front at Hinton House, Somerset

sites are all around. At least the stoppage preserved the house in its original state, so that it was an ideal location for filming the *Poldark* series for television. Sidney Godolphin's wife, Margaret, dying in London, wrote to her husband that if she might, 'I would begg that my body might lye wher I have had such a mind to goe myself, att Godolphin, among your friends. I believe, if I were carried by Sea, the expence would not be very great.' In fact, her coffin was brought home by land accompanied by a regiment of cavalry.

Part of the house dates from 1475, but much rebuilding was done before the Civil War, then in 1805 the great hall was pulled down, so that the house is no longer anything like the splendid seat of one of the Stuart kingdom's wealthiest and most powerful families, with its hundred rooms and forty chimneys built round two courtyards. The loggia of 1635 remains impressive, though, with its thick columns of granite supporting the battlemented upper wall.

Chambercombe Manor, near Ilfracombe, is no great architectural specimen, being a huddle of whitewashed buildings round a courtyard and having served as a farmhouse for a very long period. No one is very sure of its date – one book refers to fourteenth century and another to fifteenth, and the house is even reputed to date back to the twelfth, but there is little doubt that what can be seen now is not much older than the seventeenth. The name, at any rate, has ancient origins, coming from the Champernon lords of the manor in the medieval period. It is said that the farmers who occupied the house in later times were often smugglers as well.

The name is one of the most surprising things about Brickwall Manor, at Northiam in East Sussex, for this is a timber-framed house, built between 1617 and 1633, these dates appearing on the gables. But some brickwork was added later, and it is said that this was remarkable enough at the time to warrant the name of the house, though I would not have thought brick so uncommon in this part of the country by that time as to justify a name which seems so obviously perverse when you approach the front of the house. It looks modern – almost Victorian – from a distance, and in fact the chimney-stack has the date 1832 on it, but it has a symmetrical gabled Jacobean front and splendid seventeenth-century stucco ceilings inside.

Socknersh Manor at Brightling is a picturesque timber-framed house of the early years of the century, totally different in character from the untypical Slyfield Manor near Stoke d'Abernon in Surrey. The latter was built between 1625 and 1650 in the style known as 'artisan' brickwork. Some of it has since been demolished, but the main range remains, terminated at one end by a projecting wing with a Dutch gable above a curiously round-headed window and having pilasters of brick with Ionic volutes. The brick character of the house is imitated inside on the newel posts of the extraordinary staircase.

Kiplin Hall in North Yorkshire looks positively conventional by comparison with it, being a gabled three-storey patterned-brick house with a projecting tower on each of the four sides, surmounted by little domes. They were still a little on their guard in the north. The house was built about 1625 by George Calvert Baltimore, Robert Cecil's one-time secretary and founder of the State of Maryland, whose chief city is named after him. Lord Baltimore died soon after the completion of his house, which seems oddly unadventurous for the man and the time. The doorway leads into the screens passage of a conventional great hall. Perhaps it was an expression of the Puritan spirit soon to prevail over the country at large.

Slyfield Manor, Surrey

By the time the Old Hall at Youlgreave in Derbyshire was built, Charles I had been executed and Cromwell was well established as Protector. The Old Hall was small and dutifully pure, with symmetrical projecting wings, as was that at Rowsley, not far away and built two years afterwards, close to Haddon Hall, by Lady Manners' agent John Stevenson. In due course this house became the Peacock Hotel.

The so-called Castle House at Deddington, Oxfordshire, was formerly a rectorial manor house. The present building dates from around 1654 and was rebuilt from the medieval origins, of which a few details remain. The position of some of these modest Commonwealth manor houses among the ordinary houses in village streets might almost be seen as a consenting nod towards the new democracy. But among the consequences of the political upheavals of the seventeenth century was the new influence of wealthy landowners over local affairs, and from the Restoration onward the traditional power of the barons was restored even more fully than the power of the King. Some big landowners had lost property during the Commonwealth,

Milton Manor, Oxfordshire – the east front

and others had been so heavily fined that they were forced to sell large parcels of land, but they survived and mostly recovered and began to look to improvements in the quality of both their land and their homes.

At the southern end of Oxfordshire, which acquired the village from Berkshire in the recent boundary changes, is Milton Manor, built of brick after the restoration of the monarchy, for the wealthy landowner Paul Carlton. The house was quite small then, consisting of only the central block, to which the wings were added a century afterwards, with a chapel and library in the Gothick style. The library is a sign of the times, having built-in bookshelves with ogee-curved tops to match the windows. Although used now to display fine china, the shelves would have held a lot more than the mere couple of hundred books which were considered to constitute a fine library at the time when the house was built. Literacy and culture were becoming fashionable among the gentry.

Yet the times were also curiously uncouth. Gluttony and intoxication were among the gentry's ruling passions. Although domestic water-power came into its own in the latter half of the seventeenth century, with running water to bathrooms and water-closets replacing the former garderobe shoots and close-stools, there was no rapid inclination to make use of them. One of the exceptions was Shaw House, the brick mansion in Berkshire built for the Dolman family in the Elizabethan period but much altered inside during the late seventeenth and early eighteenth centuries and having running water installed on all floors. Generally, people rarely bathed and even in upper-class houses thought little of relieving themselves in a chamber-pot kept in a sideboard for the purpose, while the men drank their port at the table. Pepys once observed the Countess of Sandwich 'doing something upon the pot' in the dining-room, and it was not unusual for a visiting guest going up the grand staircase to meet a full chamber-pot coming down, in the hands of a maid who had been summoned to clear the mess by the new device of a bell-pull in every room.

Literary connections call attention to Gaulden Manor in Somerset, built early in the Restoration period. This house near Lydeard St Lawrence was built by the Turbervilles, from an older house on the site, to which James Turberville, Bishop of Exeter, is said to have retired after he had refused to take the Oath of Supremacy and been imprisoned by Elizabeth I and deprived of his see. He spent his last years in the house, and his initials are above the door between the chapel and the hall, which has the family arms above the fireplace. The old stone manor house, lying in a hidden combe among Quantock lanes, became a farmhouse in time and was known as Gaulden Farm until its rescue by its present owners.

Aynhoe Park in Northamptonshire is also largely a Restoration house, but on a rather grander scale than those mentioned hitherto. Richard Cartwright became the lord of the manor of this lovely stone village in 1615 and built an E-plan house which was, ironically as it might seem, burnt down by Royalist troops in 1645. Some of it survived, but the Cartwrights began rebuilding in the 1660s, apparently under the supervision of the King's master mason, Edward Marshall, who erected a central block of five bays between the surviving wings. Rebuilding and extending went on over many years and ended, unfortunately, with the outside of the house getting a coat of cement rendering before the Cartwright family sold the place in recent years. It has been partly converted into flats. The interior is splendid, though much later work than of the period we are discussing dominates it, some of the rooms having been designed by Sir John Soane. The hall is unmistakably an entrance hall, with a fine timber staircase.

In Shropshire, Lowe Hall and Longnor Hall date from the years of the Merry Monarch, though there is little of Merrie England to be said about Lowe Hall, at Wem, for the house was bought, along with the title of Baron of Wem, by Judge Jeffreys in the very year of the Bloody Assize, though he did not live long enough to enjoy it. Longnor Hall, near Church Stretton, was built by Sir Richard Corbett, a member of a powerful ruling family in this part of the country for hundreds of years. The brick house, however, is not large and, as with several others mentioned in the last few pages, shows how the country gentleman of the time was content with a comfortable but not opulent house, in which he no longer had to accommodate the large household of former times. Fewer servants and hangers-on were the rule, even in the palaces of great noblemen.

For the country squire, the times were difficult. If he made his living from agriculture and the rents of a few tenants, he was under economic pressure to improve his methods in order to keep up with his betters but was prevented from doing so, partly by his lack of capital and scientific knowledge and partly by the open field system of farming. And as if this was not enough, he was soon to be further impoverished by the imposition of the

Longnor Hall, Shropshire

land tax to finance the wars of William III and the Duke of Marlborough.

Capheaton Hall in Northumberland, however, illustrates a new threat from big landowners that was beginning to loom up for ordinary folk at this time – the need for a park, preferably with deer, or, at the least, extensive landscaped grounds which were now seen as a status symbol. Many small squires, getting only a few hundred pounds a year from their land in rents and produce, sold out to wealthier landowners who could afford to develop large enclosed estates on advanced agricultural principles or who derived their main incomes from industry, such as coal-mining, which was the case with the Swinburne family, one of whose descendants was the poet Algernon Charles.

Capheaton Hall was built for them in 1668. In the following century, when much baroque embroidering of the house was carried out, Lancelot Brown, a local boy who made good, was employed to do something splendid, and the 'capabilities' of the land he surveyed involved the demolition of the village where the local workers lived. True, the Swinburnes built a new model

The south door of Capheaton Hall, Northumberland

village, but this was at a time when being 'as safe as houses' was an empty phrase. So far from eating with their servants in the great hall, wealthy landowners did not even want to suffer a distant view of their servants' cottages from their drawing-room windows. The more wealth and power that came into the hands of those raised from the common people in trades and professions, the more sharply class consciousness was defined.

Buckinghamshire's manor houses of the period are still of a fairly intimate nature. The one at Bradenham is interesting on two counts apart from its architecture. Its medieval predecessor was the headquarters of the only manor in the county whose Saxon lord continued in ownership after the Conquest. I suppose we should now regard him as a collaborator. And the present house was lived in during the nineteenth century by Isaac d'Israeli, the antiquarian and father of the Prime Minister, who spent his boyhood here and got his education from his father's library in this elegant Stuart house on the large and open village green, next to the village church.

The manor house at Princes Risborough was built at the same time – about 1670 – in similar style but in a startlingly dissimilar

Bradenham, Buckinghamshire. The manor house, church and green

The gatehouse at Combe Florey, Somerset

situation, this house being in the town centre near the market-place. It has an exuberantly carved open well staircase of the kind which had become so fashionable with the increasing skills of carpenters that venerable stone stairways were often removed from old houses to make way for new wooden ones.

Long Crendon has two manor houses, as well as a surviving court house of the fifteenth century, in which the manorial courts were held. The oldest of the two houses, known as Long Crendon Manor, is on a hill above the village and has parts of a fifteenth-century house within it, including the great hall, but a great deal of modernization took place in the seventeenth and subsequent centuries. The newer manor house, built late in the Stuart period, is near the church, and this was the site of the castle owned by the manor's Norman lord, Walter Giffard, whose son became Earl of Buckingham.

The red sandstone manor house at Combe Florey, in Somerset, was built around 1675 behind a gatehouse of 1593 that originally led to a manor house standing between it and the church. Floreys, Merriets and Fraunceys were among the lords of the manor here, and there are memorials to many of them in the church, but none was half as famous as a twentieth-century resident of the manor house who liked to pose as a country squire, though he was hardly a countryman at heart and rarely went out for the sake of fresh air and exercise. Evelyn Waugh bought the old manor house at Combe Florey in 1956 and lived there until his death ten years later. Coveting a knighthood which he never got, the author of *Brideshead Revisited* would have made a less sympathetic lord of the manor than that famous novel might lead one to believe.

The seventeenth-century manor house at Wotton-under-Edge, in the Gloucestershire Cotswolds, stands on the site of the medieval Lisle Manor, which was already in ruins by the early Tudor period. It had been, intermittently, the home of the Berkeleys, those controversial lords of local manors whose inter-baronial quarrelling with the Lisles, who had claimed this manor and occupied the house, led to Viscount Lisle's death in 1470 at Nibley Green when he was trying to claim Berkeley Castle.

Lower Slaughter did not get its surviving manor house until a century after the upper village, but when it did, it got quite a house. It was built by the Cotswold master mason Valentine Strong, who was also a quarry-owner, for the Whitmore family, who held the manor for three hundred years. Some alteration has been carried out, but the house remains sturdy and individualistic, as Strong did not build to conform to the gabled Cotswold image. The date on the hall fireplace is 1658. The rooms have fine plaster ceilings, and the house is reached from the village street via huge gate piers of stone. There is also a stone dovecote which predates the house and is also massive, with an entrance like that of a house between gables.

Hidcote Manor, better known for Major Lawrence Johnston's splendid gardens than for the house itself, was built late in the seventeenth century but much altered afterwards. It is an attractive house of Cotswold limestone, unlike Eye Manor in Hereford & Worcester, built around the same time in brick, and more attractive within than without. This house was built for Ferdinando Gorges, a retired Barbados sugar merchant and slave-trader who was known as the 'King of the Black Market'. The outstanding attractions of the house are the gorgeously decorated plaster ceilings, with fruit and flowers, cherubs and mythological figures. The present owners are Mr and Mrs

Honington Hall, Warwickshire

Christopher Sandford, one-time owners of the Golden Cockerell Private Press. Much influenced by William Morris, they produced fine books which included the log of the *Bounty*. Many private press books are on display in the house.

In Warwickshire, Honington Hall, near Shipston-on-Stour, is also a merchant's house and was also built of brick, only two years after Eye Manor, but what a difference there is between them! Sir Henry Parker built himself this house which is stylish outside and sumptuous inside, though a good deal of the interior attraction was added by a later owner, Joseph Townsend. An earlier house had stood here, and its dovecote and stables survive. Although the main block is symmetrical, with busts of emperors in niches above the ground-floor windows, the obsession with symmetry had passed by the time much of the work at Honington was done, and there is some relief in seeing odd arches, gateways and walls attached to the house and leading to the gardens. The interior decoration is excellent, with much stucco relief, and one is led to reflect here on how far the wealthy landowner had come, in standards of taste and

The staircase hall at Honington

comfort, if not in personal power and glory, in a matter of three hundred years.

Back to Hereford & Worcester, where a house at Much Marcle, known as Hellens, although principally Jacobean, seems to have originated at an earlier date, for Mary Tudor's initials are on an overmantel. The Walwyn lords of the manor were Roman Catholics, and it was Fulke Walwyn who rebuilt or modernized the house around 1641, building an octagonal brick dovecote outside at the same time. Though brick-built, the house has mullioned and transomed windows. A tower at the back has a stone newel staircase, but Walwyn added a wooden staircase, as well as fine ceilings and a chimney-piece thought to be the work of the local craftsman John Abel, who was entitled the King's Carpenter in 1645 for building a powder-mill during the siege of Hereford. The house is a trifle dilapidated, tucked away at the end of a village lane.

The old hall at Newbold Verdon, in Leicestershire, is of late seventeenth-century date, but the manor is of ancient foundation, taking its name from the French town of Verdun, whence came the Norman lords of the manor. They were followed by Hastings, Devereux and Crews, and Sir Thomas Crew was among the first baronets created by James I. A later Crew, by which time the family had been ennobled with a barony, was the first peer of the realm to be also a bishop, as well as lord of the manor, and he bequeathed the estate to a nephew through whom it came into the possession of Edward the husband of Lady Mary Wortley Montagu, who described the house as 'one of the most charming and pleasant places I ever saw', though she mocked the 'honest English squire, who verily believes the Greek wines less delicious than March beer . . .'.

The hard Millstone Grit farther north does not lend itself to intricate carving, and Eyam Hall in Derbyshire, built a little earlier and dutifully symmetrical, is a gaunt-looking building in the village street, with odd triangular gables projecting above mullioned windows as if they were added as an afterthought to break the straight roof-line. The village stocks stand near the house, but the lord of the manor who put miserable wrongdoers in them would have lived at the older manor house, Bradshaw Hall, of which little now survives. Eyam Hall was built ten years after the tragic visitation of the plague which made the village famous through the heroic but possibly misguided self-sacrifice of its inhabitants.

Richard Graham, the first Viscount Preston, who rebuilt the

The entrance Hall at Nunnington, North Yorkshire

fine country house of brick at Norton Conyers, near Ripon, seems also to have done much remodelling at Nunnington Hall, farther east on Yorkshire's limestone belt, where he spent the last few years of his life. The grey house is something of an architectural puzzle, but it has some attractive Jacobean details, including a fine oak open-well staircase and carved chimney-pieces.

Sewerby Hall, now in Humberside, was built about 1714, a characteristic house of the period, belonging to the Graeme family, but now rather anachronistic a few yards away from Bridlington's seaside amusements. Its front is rendered and painted white, and it is very difficult to visualize this as a Jacobean manor house, before seaside resorts had acquired any kind of popularity and the lord's interest was still in making capital from his tenants. Nowadays, it has a miniature railway and what might be called a miniature zoo, where the beach donkeys are housed – one of the more unusual uses to which manor house buildings have finally come.

Capheaton Hall, which we have already noticed in North-

Wallington Hall, Northumberland. Stone heads brought from London's Aldersgate,
demolished in 1761

umberland, was followed in twenty years, and only a stone's
throw away, by Wallington Hall, with which Sir William Blackett, a mining and shipping magnate, upstaged the Swinburnes
down the road. The age of luxuries had well and truly arrived by
this time, even in the far north. On the site of an older tower
house, built on to an earlier pele tower, where – once again –
'Capability' Brown was to carry out some work on the grounds
later, Sir William built his Italianate mansion, which was altered
and extended by his son, also Sir William, in the following
century. The story goes that the last member of the family which
had owned the tower-house, Sir John Fenwick, owned a fine
horse called White Sorrel, and when Sir John was executed for
his part in the assassination plot against William III, the King
took White Sorrel for himself, and it was this horse he was riding
when it stumbled on a molehill and threw him, causing his death
a few days later.

The house is of warm-coloured local sandstone, and inside
there are marble fireplaces, fine plasterwork and mural paint-

ings done much later under the influence of Ruskin, by which time the house was the property of the Trevelyans, who entertained many literary and artistic guests here as well as spawning famous historians. But Reynolds' portrait of Sir William Blackett in the Saloon seems to preside over the house still, and it was he who built the village of Cambo in a paternalistic venture for the workers on his estate; a gesture which the earlier lords of the manor would scarcely have understood.

By the time Gunby Hall was built in Lincolnshire, William and Mary were on the English thrones. Sir Joshua Reynolds is represented here, too, though the place is hardly as grand as Wallington. Indeed, it is rather plain, built of brick with stone dressings on three storeys for Sir William Massingberd, whose descendants continued to own it until recent years through the female line, one of the females having been a well-known campaigner for women's rights – Emily Caroline Massingberd, whose singularly apt name for such a cause has an intimidating ring about it.

The Old Manor at West Allington, near the county's border with Leicestershire, is an earlier house, built in the Restoration period, and being on Lincolnshire's narrow stone belt, is in warm Liassic limestone. The front has Dutch gables and a curious arrangement of windows with mullions and transoms. Only minor alterations have been done here since the house was first built, and it has been restored in recent years after standing empty for nearly a century.

Back in the south, Antony House in Cornwall was begun in Queen Anne's time but not completed until George I was on the throne. Once again, Sir Joshua Reynolds appears among the fashionable acquisitions of the house's earlier owners. They were the Carew family, who had owned land here since Elizabethan days, some of their monuments being in the village church. It was Sir William Carew who built the present grand mansion, of the local grey Pentewan stone, an igneous rock harder than granite, which explains why there is no exterior decorative detail.

The Carews became by marriage with the Pole family whose ancient manor house at Shute, in neighbouring Devon, we noticed in an earlier chapter. One of the Carews had been among Charles I's judges, but another was executed by Cromwell when his loyalties wavered. His portrait is in the library, and stitches can be seen where the canvas was put back in its frame after being removed in disgust by Sir Alexander's relations when he changed sides. The later Carew Poles added extensions here in brick. The interior is not exactly sumptuous either, the panelling of Dutch oak making the rooms rather sombre, but the grounds, thought to have been designed by Humphrey Repton, are splendid, with fine specimen trees.

A well-to-do landlord's house by this time might consist of almost any permutation from the variety of purpose-built rooms invented by social need and architectural imagination: entrance hall, drawing-room, saloon, study, library, morning room, music room, billiard room, smoking-room, breakfast room, dining-room, parlour, ante-chamber, dressing-rooms, bedrooms and nursery, kitchen, laundry room, pantry and scullery, conservatory and servants' hall, and what have you. Domestic chapels were rarer now, though some wealthy houses still had them. The 'saloon' might serve as a ballroom, when occasion demanded, or as a gallery in which the family pictures and *objets d'art* were displayed. Only the higher aristocracy would have any comprehensive range of all these options, but the well-established country gentleman now lived well, in spite of the economic pressures upon him, and if he did not spend his time in cultural pursuits, as perhaps only a few did, then he pursued instead the fox or the hare, as often as not in the company of the village parson, who might owe his living to the lord of the manor and was a Tory like his master, who still presided over manorial courts in places where local magistrates had not yet been appointed and who sat in Parliament with the support of all those voters who knew which side their bread was buttered on, whatever they might think of his lordship in private.

The wealthier lords who owned large estates provided housing for their workers, sometimes building model villages, not always from entirely altruistic motives, as we have already seen, although in Leicestershire Shuckburgh Ashby of Quenby Hall was said to have built Hungarton from 'a principle laudable and truly disinterested', and Francis Edwards had to mortgage his own house to finance the rebuilding of Welham in about 1720. We have already noticed Chenies in Buckinghamshire, and the Russell earls of Bedford built there one of the best early 'model villages' for their estate workers in the first half of the nineteenth century, by which time other paternal landlords were following suit. Too often, though, new houses were built only to replace those demolished by the lord of the manor to make way for his landscaped park, as at Wall in Lincolnshire, begun in 1725 by

James Bateman, whose Wellvale House had been provided with a series of lakes, and nothing but a remodelled church remained where the former villagers had once lived and moved and had their being.

CHAPTER 7

Decline and Fall

Edward Gibbon spent much of his early life at Buriton Manor in Hampshire, the estate of his father, a country gentleman and Member of Parliament. The house had been built in the early Georgian years, on to an older house which Gibbon described as 'an old mansion in a state of decay', in a spot 'not happily chosen, at the end of a village and the bottom of a hill', and when Gibbon senior died, leaving the estate to his son, it was a financial embarrassment to him. The place was eventually taken over by farmers and declined to its former state of decay once again.

The demise of the manor house as an institution was in process generally, as well as in this particular case. Whilst Gibbon was a boy, Parliament passed an Act which made 'lord of the manor' an adventitious title. An 'esquire' was a man who acquired one manor, or estate; a man who owned two was entitled 'knight', and anyone with more than two became a baron. It was only two years afterwards, in 1746, when the last remnants of the old feudal loyalties in Britain were beaten to death in battle, with Cumberland's massacre of Bonnie Prince Charlie's army at Culloden.

The ideal of the country squire at the beginning of the eighteenth century, now exercising – along with the village parson – a more paternalistic authority over villagers, tenants and estate workers, was Sir Roger de Coverley, Joseph Addison's fictitious friend of ancient Worcestershire stock. In church, Sir Roger was almost as much a father to his flock as the parson: 'As Sir Roger is Landlord to the whole Congregation, he keeps them in very good Order, and will suffer no Body to sleep in it besides himself; . . . sometimes, when he is pleased with the Matter of his Devotion, he pronounces Amen three or four times to the same Prayer; and sometimes stands up when every Body else is upon their Knees, to count the Congregation, or see if any of his Tenants are missing.' In the court, Sir Roger was anxious for justice to be seen to be done and would not ride roughshod over

Harlaxton Manor, Lincolnshire

anyone's rights, even in the most trivial matters: 'My Friend Sir
Roger heard them both, upon a round Trot; and after having
paused some Time, told them, with the Air of a Man who would
not give his Judgment rashly, that much might be said on both
Sides.' In the hunting field, Sir Roger had been indefatigable,
and he had a house full of trophies of the chase, though as 'old
Age came on, he left off Fox-hunting; but a Hare is not yet safe
that sits within ten miles of his House'.

As to the house, it stood near a ruined abbey, haunted by a
headless horse which Sir Roger's butler was careful to warn the
squire's guests about. Sir Roger had a gallery hung with portraits
of his ancestors, whose histories he knew in detail. His domestic
staff included a groom and a coachman, and a resident chaplain,
and he dined frequently on gifts of fish or game brought him by
his tenants.

But the passing of the squirearchy's great days and the growing urban view of its representatives as rustic eccentrics are well
expressed by Addison, when Sir Roger is making a journey by
boat on the Thames:

> I do not remember I have any where mentioned, in Sir Roger's Character, his
> Custom of saluting every Body that passes by him with a Good-morrow, or a
> Good-night. This the old Man does out of the Overflowings of his Humanity
> though at the same time it renders him so popular among all his Country
> Neighbours, that it is thought to have gone a good way in making him once
> or twice Knight of the Shire. He cannot forbear this Exercise of Benevolence
> even in Town, when he meets with any one in his Morning or Evening Walk.
> It broke from him to several Boats that passed by us upon the Water; but, to
> the Knight's great Surprize, as he gave the Good-night to two or three young
> Fellows a little before our Landing, one of them instead of returning the
> Civility, asked us what queer old Putt we had in the Boat; and whether he
> was not ashamed to go Wenching at his Years? with a great deal of the like
> Thames-Ribaldry. Sir Roger seemed a little shocked at first, but at length
> assuming a Face of Magistracy, told us, That if he were a Middlesex Justice,
> he would make such Vagrants know that her Majesty's Subjects, were no
> more to be abused by Water than by Land.

This idealized version of the eighteenth-century squire, with
higher moral instincts than had ruled the country districts of
England before, was not wholly divorced from reality – in a few
cases, at any rate. Take, for instance, Squire Cradock of Gumley

Hall in Leicestershire. He was not, it is true, a keen sportsman, being more interested in the arts and having a fine library, but he was 'respected by people of all parties for his worth, and idolised by the poor for his benevolence'. He had come into a fortune on the death of his father and become a man of fashion, spending much time in London and numbering among his friends Dr Johnson and David Garrick. He became a Fellow of the Society of Arts and built Gumley Hall in 1764, of brick with a stone colonnade. Here he entertained Garrick and possibly Johnson, although Mrs Cradock, very sensibly, had been heard to say that news of Dr Johnson's approach would also signal her imminent departure. The house cost Joseph Cradock £8,000, and his gardens were laid out so well that they became one of the county's showplaces. But Squire Cradock ran into debt through lavish spending and had to sell his library and his estate. By this time, however, he was over eighty and an invalid, living princi-pally on 'turnips, roasted apples and coffee'. He confided to a friend that he had entertained two of the most absurd notions in the world. One was that independence was honourable, and the other that literature was its own reward.

At Quatt, on the eastern outskirts of Shropshire, Dudmaston Hall, a red brick house with stone dressings, had been 'lately rebuilt' in 1730. This had for long been the manor house of the Wolryche family, and we can see in the monument to Lady Mary Wolryche in the village church the same aspirations to culture among some, at least, of the ruling classes. Lady Mary, who died in 1678, is shown reclining a trifle uncomfortably and holding a lute in her left hand. She looks, as I have remarked elsewhere, as if she wishes she could play the damn thing, but that is the sculptor's fault, not hers.

Then there was Squire Cotton, Izaak Walton's amiable com-panion, whose Beresford Hall at Alstonefield, in Staffordshire, was demolished a century ago, though the fishing-lodge he built beside the River Dove in 1674 is still standing, with his own and Walton's initials intertwined over the doorway. The village church still has the Cotton family box pew, though Charles Cotton himself was scarcely a pious father of his flock like Sir Roger de Coverley, having been a roisterer in his younger days, ending up in debt like Joseph Cradock. But he was a scholar, too, who translated Montaigne and wrote other books as well as the sequel to Walton's famous work on Angling. And he was a man of infectious happiness and charming naïvety, who once claimed to have let a mile of rope down the awesome Eldon Hole without touching bottom! Even his creditors could scarcely bring themselves to judge him harshly.

Landowners such as these were the exception rather than the rule, however. Many of them now were men who had not the least professional interest in agriculture but saw the ownership of a considerable estate in terms of their social standing. They might be merchants or industrial magnates, who coveted land as they coveted pretentious coats of arms, nicely satirized by Thomas Love Peacock in *Crotchet Castle*: 'Arms, three empty bladders turgescent, to show how opinions are formed; three bags of gold, pendent, to show why they are maintained; three naked swords, trenchant, to show how they are administered; and three barbers' blocks, gaspant, to show how they are swallowed.' Often enough, these men were unlearned local despots, squabbling over their territorial rights, like the Corbets and the Needhams of Shropshire's Adderley Park and Shavington Hall respectively. The Corbets were Protestant and Parliamentarians, the Needhams Catholic and Royalists, and their neighbouring estates were already engaged in long-standing and idiotic rivalry when the Civil War came, bringing an undignified squabble over the parish church and, indeed, in it. Neither squire, villagers nor tenants profited from this ridiculous feudal farce, and the passage of time brought a plague on both their houses, one being demolished and the other abandoned to dereliction.

Some landowners were so concerned at the way the wind was blowing for them that they wanted to turn the clock back. John Perceval, Earl of Egmont in the Irish peerage, MP for Bridgwater in Somerset, and father of the Prime Minister, Spencer Perceval, actually tried to bring in an Act of Parliament reviving feudal tenures. He did not succeed, of course. The English may be slow to adapt to changes for the better, but they do not readily march backward to changes for the worse.

Meanwhile, the landed gentry and even the *nouveaux riches* industrialists were building country homes which they liked to think of as manor houses, even if they did not actually call them such, and in which they now had the luxury of upholstered furniture. One house that *was* called such was Combe Hay Manor House, built around 1730 in the county where John Perceval was to pursue his feudal fantasies in the building of a pseudo-baronial castle at Enmore. Combe Hay is an elegant Georgian mansion built of Bath stone close to the village church, with lawns sloping down to an ornamental lake.

One of the new fashions of the time was for grounds enhanced by romantic ruins, and these were often specially erected by artful landscape gardeners, at great expense, and thus became known as 'follies' by common-sense folk. The ruins at Stratton Park, in Hampshire, however, are real enough – the remaining portico of the house built in 1803 by Sir Thomas Baring, whose wife Cobbett took to task rather unfairly when he saw a number of little girls dressed in camlet gowns, white aprons and plaid cloaks, one of whom told him that Lady Baring had given her the clothes and taught her to read and sing hymns. This launched Cobbett into a sermon on the hypocrisy of the upper classes who become charitable to save their own souls. They also, it must be said, helped to bring new fashions and modern comforts to the benighted and slow-moving rural areas.

Kinlet Hall, in Shropshire, however, is another of those cases where the local squire built his house at the expense of the villagers, for he completely demolished the old village to make way for his large park and built a small estate village well out of sight of his drawing-room windows, diverting the road to leave just the church with his house in the park. The Childe family were the culprits here. One might say the villagers had the last laugh, for the brick house eventually became the village school, but they had a long time to wait for this, and all over the country at this period landlords were inventing the compulsory purchase order – without compensation – in the interests of feathering their own nests.

In North Yorkshire, Sir Thomas Robinson's fine house at Rokeby was complete by 1731, a five-bay front of stone with rendering on the other sides and a courtyard at one of them. The house had an entrance hall, library, breakfast room, dining-room etc on the ground floor, and in the saloon above an inscription read '*Fay ce que voudras*' – the same motto from Rabelais which the Hell Fire Club had over its entrance at Medmenham soon afterwards – 'Do as you please.' Sir Thomas Robinson had bought the Rokeby estate in 1720, and eight years later he married the Earl of Carlisle's daughter, through whom the property duly passed to the Howards.

Sir Walter Scott used Rokeby as the setting for his Civil War poem of that name, enlisting the then owner, his friend J. B. S. Morritt, to provide him with local colour and background information, but it is with a far greater work of art that Rokeby Hall will for long be associated, for it was John Morritt who purchased a painting by Velasquez which had been brought to

England from Spain early in the nineteenth century – *The Toilet of Venus*. You could hardly get farther from the musty old tapestries of earlier manor house walls than this voluptuous nude. It was painted to be seen at close quarters, and it hung at Rokeby for nearly a hundred years. When it was sold in 1906, the National Gallery bought it for £45,000, by which time it had become well known as the *Rokeby Venus*.

Also in Yorkshire, George III's Surveyor-General, Sir Thomas Worsley, built himself a splendid mansion of limestone, with a park and a riding-school, on a spot at Hovingham where a Roman villa had once stood. The centre of the house was the ballroom on the upper floor, reached by an open-well staircase which was given an iron balustrade later. But the building's chief feature is still the riding school with stables, reached through an archway with a tunnel-vaulted roof.

The seat of the Danby family near Masham, Swinton Hall, was rebuilt around 1800 by James Wyatt, for William Danby, who gave unemployed local men a shilling a day to build his splendid folly, the so-called 'Druid's Temple' on the moors nearby. The men were thus not made to feel they were receiving charity, and Danby got what is undoubtedly one of the outstanding mock ruins in Britain.

Croxdale Hall, near Spennymoor in Durham, was built around 1760 for General Salvin on the site of an earlier house where the Salvins had long been lords of the manor. The medieval church, now derelict, stood near by. The Salvins had never gone in for ostentation, for the present house is called 'plain, honest' by Pevsner, and the hall of their old house had been furnished only with 'one cupboard, one table, two buffet stools, and one chair' towards the end of Elizabeth's reign. Perhaps the family's austere surroundings infected the General's son with a passion for revolt, for Anthony Salvin was the architect of Harlaxton Hall, of which more shortly.

Ormesby Hall, now in Cleveland, was built in the mid-eighteenth century by the Pennymans, who had owned the estate since the Tudor period. The house is plain on the outside, but the interior has good chimney-pieces and stucco ceilings, and a fine gallery, while in Cumbria, Dalemain, seen from the road from Ullswater to Penrith, near Dacre, was built at about the same time by Sir Edward Hasell, though the long Georgian front was a later addition, and parts of an older house were incorporated in the building – the former hall and a newel staircase remaining there. The front is faced with ashlared grey limestone quarried locally. Sir Edward was Steward to Lady Anne Clifford, the Earl of Cumberland's daughter, who was almost a rival to Bess of Hardwick in the extent of her building activities. She died in 1676, the last of the line, and Hasell bought the Dalemain estate four years later, since when the family has been in continuous occupation, owning much of the land round Ullswater.

The Blundell family's manor house, at Ince Blundell in Lancashire, is a rather heavy-handed Georgian mansion built on to a sixteenth-century house, the Blundells having been lords of the manor since the thirteenth century. It is an interesting commentary on the changed character of wealthy landlords that by the time of the new house, or at any rate soon after, the family were building classical temples and monuments in the grounds, and eventually Henry Blundell built an impressive domed Pantheon to house his collection of antique sculpture. This, however, was subsequently sold to Liverpool Corporation – a more recent sign of the times.

In Buckinghamshire, meanwhile, the heirs of the great John Hampden were pulling down his ancient house in a quiet corner of the Chiltern Hills and building a new mansion, though some small details of the medieval one were left. The new house was mainly an exercise in Gothic Revival architecture, with battlements and ogee-headed windows, reached from a gateway flanked by curiously shaped lodges known locally as the 'pepper pots'. This house, too, was provided with stables in matching style but is now a girls' school.

Also in the Chilterns, Charles Savage bought the estate of Hughenden in 1738 and converted a farmhouse into his residence, at the same time creating a beautiful park on sloping ground from the arable land around it. In 1847, this brick house was purchased by Benjamin Disraeli, and he and his wife converted it into an unattractive Victorian house. Disraeli lived there until his death, and the place, owned by the National Trust, is largely preserved as a Disraeli museum.

The Drake family had been the local squires at Amersham for three hundred years when Shardeloes was built outside the town for them in 1758–66. William Drake was then the local MP. His architect was Stiff Leadbetter, but Robert Adam and James Wyatt both had their hands in the building later, and Humphrey Repton laid out the grounds. 'Mr. Drake's is a very beautiful place,' wrote William Cobbett, 'and has a great deal of very fine timber upon it. I think I counted pretty nearly 200 oak trees,

Hughenden Manor, Buckinghamshire

worth, on an average, five pounds apiece, growing within twenty yards of the road I was going along.' That, too, was a sign of the times – the value of the trees in aesthetic terms was second to their price in economic terms. The Drake of Cobbett's time was Thomas, who would have appealed to Cobbett if he had known him, for when the Penny Post in 1841 required houses to have numbers on their doors, Drake flatly refused to have London dictating what he did with *his* houses! London lived longer than the Drakes, however, and Shardeloes was converted into luxury flats for well-off London commuters.

Over in Herefordshire, Berrington Hall, on the Leominster-Ludlow road, was built for the banker Thomas Harley, a Lord Mayor of London by the time he was thirty-seven, whose local antecedents drew him back to this part of the country to establish his seat on a site chosen with the help of 'Capability' Brown, who designed the grounds before the house was built. Henry Holland, Brown's son-in-law, was the architect, and the sandstone house has hardly been altered inside, though much of the outside stonework has been replaced. There are fine chimney-

Shardeloes, Buckinghamshire: now luxury flats

pieces, painted friezes and plaster ceilings in the house, which
also has a courtyard at the back with laundry, kitchen, dairy,
bakery and servants' quarters round it.

The most splendid part of Berrington is the Staircase Hall in
the centre of the house, with a stair rail of bronze, Corinthian
marble columns and a glass dome above the landing. The library
has medallions of writers on the ceiling, terminating appropriately with Addison. But perhaps the most curious aspect of the
place, now owned by the National Trust, is the throw-back in
interior decoration to the oldest manor houses we have seen, for
on some of the walls are fine tapestries, woven at the beginning
of the present century, when the Cawley family were in possession. Sir Frederick and Lady Cawley lost two sons in the First
World War, and the surviving son, who became the second Lord
Cawley, lost his own son in the Second. The Dowager Lady
Cawley lived here until 1978.

At Stanford-on-Teme, the Winnington family became owners
of the manor at the end of the seventeenth century through
marriage with the heiress of the previous owners, the Salway

Berrington Hall, Hereford & Worcester

family, who had been there for hundreds of years. Monuments to both families are in the parish church. Cobbett visited Sir Thomas Winnington MP in 1826, admiring the park and its fine trees and noting a laudable feature inside the house: 'Sir Thomas was out shooting; but he soon came home, and gave us a very polite reception. I had time, yesterday, to see the place, to look at trees, and the like, and I wished to get away early this morning; but being prevailed on to stay to breakfast, here I am, at six o'clock in the morning, in one of the best and best-stocked private libraries that I ever saw; and, what is more, the owner, from what passed yesterday, when he brought me hither, convinced me that he was acquainted with the *insides* of the books.' Sixty years after Cobbett's visit, however, the house was severely damaged by fire, and extensive rebuilding had to be carried out.

The so-called manor house at Stoke d'Abernon in Surrey contains what Pevsner describes as a 'pot-pourri of C18 details in various styles, none remarkable'. This brick house was built around 1760 from an older house near the River Mole, where Sir John d'Abernon had been lord of the manor in the thirteenth century and whose brass in the village church is the oldest in England.

Rather less entitled to the name of Manor House is Pitzhanger, at Ealing. This house was built by Sir John Soane in 1802, for his own use, from an earlier house, though he sold it within ten years. Portland stone emphasizes the monumental conception of what was actually a modest-sized house, in what was then a country parish outside London. The classical façade has four Ionic columns supporting statues. The house had the almost obligatory billiard room on the first floor, as well as front and back parlours, and in a courtyard at the back Sir John had fragments of classical ruins, part of his fashionable collection which formed the museum named after him at his later house in Lincoln's Inn Fields. Pitzhanger Manor duly became the Ealing Public Library.

All this backward-looking building activity by prosperous gentlemen in the south was more than matched by a positively pseudo-feudal family at the other end of the country, the Lowthers, who had been lords of extensive manors over large parts of Cumbria since the fourteenth century, rivalling Percys and Howards in the vastness of their estates. They demolished the ancient village of Lowther in the course of building their mansion with its large park. They erected a new estate village named

Pitzhanger House, Ealing: now the public library

Newtown, well out of sight of the house, which was built partly from the stone of the ruined Shap Abbey, also owned by the family, who became viscounts and earls of Lonsdale. Between 1806 and 1811 they built a new mansion on the site of their earlier manor house destroyed by fire. It was a sham-Gothic pile called Lowther Castle, designed by Robert Smirke and a fitting expression of the Lowthers' empire-building capitalism. But early in the twentieth century the family abandoned the place as being beyond upkeep, and it fell into ruin. It is now a mere shell, roofless and empty, like a redundant film set left here by Metro-Goldwyn-Mayer. It seems a fitting epitaph to baronial aspirations in a democratic society, for it was soon after its abandonment that Parliament finally abolished, in the Law of Property Acts in the 1920s, the last remnants of manorial rights and procedures which had continued to crop up intermittently in the nineteenth century.

If the manorial song was ended, however, the melody lingered on. Lincolnshire expresses the point well enough in Bayons Manor, now, like Lowther, a ruin. It was built by Charles

Tennyson, uncle of the poet and himself a politician aspiring to a peerage he never got. He compensated by building Bayons, modestly enough at first but eventually becoming carried away by baronial romance and turning the house into a flamboyant mock-Tudor 'castle', with a keep and a great hall, within inner and outer baileys. All this began about 1835, when Tennyson uncovered, or invented, an ancient family lineage called d'Eyncourt. Within a century, the place was a ruin.

Even more of an exercise in megalomania is Salvin's Harlaxton Manor in the same county, although George de Ligne Gregory's lineage was at least genuine, if not noble. Harlaxton is a baroque extravaganza such as a real lord of the manor in earlier times would have thought fit for Kubla Khan, in style as well as size. Mr Gregory was merely landed gentry, but he had a vast art collection and built this monstrous pile to house it – a caricature of Tudor building. Every architectural device known to man seems to have been incorporated in the effort to make a visual impact – bridge, gatehouse, gazebos, towers, turrets, cupolas, gables, oriels, balustrades, arcades, terraces, mullions and transoms all combine to create the theatrical effect of the outside, whilst within, lavish decoration imparts a dream-world image to the house whose empty rooms and corridors, deprived of their intended contents, now echo like the vast halls of *Citizen Kane* and house, appropriately enough, the University of Evansville, from Indiana, USA. The wonder is that the place was not shipped across the Atlantic to Hollywood.

Harlaxton was built in the 1830s, and further flights of the Victorian fancy for medieval mansions soon followed. Canford Manor in Dorset and Minley Manor in Hampshire are roughly of the same time – mid-century – and the same striving for opulence by the *nouveaux riches*. Minley Manor, near Farnborough, is a brick-built *château*-style mansion built for the banker Raikes Currie who, being a Catholic, had a private chapel in it.

It was only recently, however, that William Cobbett, travelling along the valley of Hampshire's Avon, had deplored the loss of so many manor houses:

> Every parish had its manor-house in the first place; and then there were, down this valley, twenty-one others; so that, in this distance of about thirty miles, there stood fifty mansion-houses. Where are they *now*. I believe there are but eight that are at all worthy of the name . . . In several places I saw, still remaining, indubitable traces of an ancient manor-house, namely a

dove-cote or pigeon-house. The poor pigeons have kept possession of their heritage, from generation to generation . . . while the paper money system has swept away, or rather swallowed-up, the owners of the dove-cotes . . . about forty families of which owners have been ousted in this one valley, and have become dead-weight creatures, tax-gatherers, barrack-fellows, thief-takers, or, perhaps, paupers or thieves.

Canford, now the well-known boys' school, was originally the manor house of Lord de Mauley, but in 1846 it was purchased by an iron-master from Merthyr Tydfil, Sir John Guest, who employed Sir Charles Barry to transform it into the spectacular mock-Tudor towered and turreted pleasure-dome whose treasures, like Harlaxton's, did not remain there a hundred years, many of them having gone to New York's Metropolitan Museum. Sir John and Lady Charlotte's initials are well represented in the house, but the only genuine medieval bit of Canford is the huge oblong kitchen, called John of Gaunt's Kitchen (though the Duke of Lancaster never owned it) and having its original louvred chimneys in projecting chimney-breasts.

So-called manor houses continued to be built throughout the Victorian period, not all as flamboyant as Harlaxton and others we have noticed but most of them coming, if not actually to dust, then at least to rather sub-baronial uses within decades rather than centuries. The self-exaltation of their builders, so short-lived, demonstrated their dealings in stocks and shares rather than in the lives and deaths of men dependent on the land.

The case of Witley Park, near Godalming in Surrey, is typical. It was built in mock-Tudor style for half a million pounds by Whitaker Wright, the financier, in about 1900. It was called Lea Park then and had grounds extending to 3,500 acres. Wright had extensive mining interests and a streak of megalomania. A billiard room with a glass-domed roof, underneath a lake, was one of his more extravagant fantasies. But hardly was the house completed before he was brought to trial on a charge of fraud and sentenced to seven years penal servitude, and in 1904 he committed suicide by poisoning himself. His gravestone in the local churchyard describes him as 'Lord of the Manor of Witley' and says that he loved the poor! The house itself was gutted in 1952 and then completely demolished at the end of a half-century which had seen many real manor houses disappear as a result of death duties or redevelopment plans. Ragdale Hall in Leicestershire, Wingerworth Hall in Derbyshire, Rolleston Hall

Canford Manor, Dorset – now a boys' school

in Staffordshire, Agecroft Hall in Lancashire and Sprotborough Hall in Yorkshire are just a handful of the historic houses we have lost.

The nation's wealth and power may have passed in the nineteenth century from the upper classes in the country to the professional classes in the towns, and the ideal of an upright gentleman now was one who served the public from altruistic motives, rather than one who expected the public to serve him, but the old notions were slow to collapse, as is shown by those sycophantic Victorian volumes on county 'leaders' which tended to class the subjects first by their rank, second by their staunch Conservatism, and third by their upright church-manship. These lost leaders were set up on pedestals to be admired more for their packaging than their content, like the merchandise in supermarkets. Such a volume on Hertfordshire, for instance, published in 1894, describes Ralph Branton Day Esq. JP as having the characteristic tastes and instincts of a British squire, and invites our admiration for them. 'For the past seven and twenty years he has annually spent two or three months in Scotland, grouse shooting and fishing.' Mr Day's Hertfordshire estate was Micklefield Hall. Joseph Grout Williams Esq. JP, 'one of the principal landowners in the neighbourhood of Tring, and Lord of the Manor of Pendley', was said to be 'a very kind and generous landlord. He spends a great deal of time, as well as money, in improving his property, and promoting the interests of the tenantry, whose love and respect he has gained in a singularly high degree. In various respects Mr. Williams has been a great benefactor to the poor on his estates, and has helped in every way to brighten their lives and to make their lot lighter and pleasanter.'

Note how it is taken for granted that the poor are a part of the natural order. Pendley Manor had its origins in the fifteenth century, when Sir Robert Whittingham enclosed two hundred acres of land, pulling down the houses of a town or large village which had tailors and shoemakers and at least thirteen ploughs, seizing the tenants' land and building a mansion there with pasture for his livestock, forcing the peasants whose families had lived there for generations to move elsewhere. The present house, rebuilt in the 1870s, is now an adult education centre.

Another of Salvin's *tours de force* was Muncaster Castle in Cumbria. Parts of a former castle, including a pele tower, were neatly incorporated in this mansion built in 1866 for Lord Muncaster, whose family, the Penningtons, had been lords of the manor for centuries and still live there today. The place is famous for the so-called Luck of Muncaster, a glass drinking-bowl supposedly presented to Sir John Pennington for giving refuge to the fugitive King Henry VI in 1463. The battlemented modern house was built in pink granite and has fine chimney-pieces but is more widely known for its beautiful gardens and their views of the Lake District hills.

Other Victorian 'manor houses' included Whatton Manor in Nottinghamshire, a mock-Tudor mansion built by the 'lord of the manor' Mr T. Dickinson Hall, in 1840. Then there was Waddesdon Manor, in Buckinghamshire, another French *château*, completed in 1880 for Baron Ferdinand de Rothschild, of which *Country Life* said: 'Its lofty tourelles and skyward elaborations might well be lifted above the swelling foliage of thick woods in Touraine.' But Mr Gladstone's daughter was more impressed by the fact that 'there is not a book in the house save 20 improper French novels'.

And there was Wightwick Manor, built between 1887 and 1893 for Theodore Mander, the paint manufacturer, and handed

Muncaster Castle, Cumbria

over to the National Trust within forty-five years. It is a part-brick and part-timbered place with many gables and ornamental chimneys, and a great hall or parlour rising through two storeys, all now preserved as a Pre-Raphaelite museum, with wallpaper and tapestries by William Morris, stained-glass windows by Kempe, pictures by Burne-Jones and others of the fraternity, and a garden by Alfred Parsons.

Whilst Wightwick Manor was in process of building, the government of Robert Cecil, third Marquess of Salisbury, brought in the Local Government Act of 1888, establishing county and borough councils, soon to be followed by urban and rural councils, and putting the final nail in the coffin of rural administration and justice by the private gentry. The 'squire' had become an anachronism, continuing to live in the big house in the style to which centuries of tradition had accustomed him, though with a somewhat depleted retinue, hanging on to his courtesy title like a retired military man still using his rank but having as little authority over people's lives – except in his imagination, as he rode to hounds, presided over the village

Waddesdon Manor, Buckinghamshire – the south front

flower show, presented the prize for the largest onion and sat in the VIP pew at church.

His declined circumstances provided novelists of the nineteenth and early twentieth centuries with material for fine passages of prose, to be found in Dickens and Trollope, George Eliot and Mary Webb, generally musing on the personality and habits of a man out of touch with his time; as well as mockery of his pretensions in such names as Peacock's 'Headlong Hall' and 'Chainmail Hall', and Priestley's 'Blessem Hall'; whilst non-fiction writers such as Cobbett reflected more on the consequences of his passing for the quality of rural life.

As for his house, however, we may perhaps return to Thomas Love Peacock, who describes the situation of Mr Crotchet's home thus:

He was not without a plausible pretence for styling his villa a castle, for, in its immediate vicinity, and within his own enclosed domain, were the manifest traces, on the brow of the hill, of a Roman station, or *castellum*, which was still called the Castle by the country people. The primitive mounds and

Wightwick Manor, West Midlands – the south front

trenches, merely overgrown with greensward, with a few patches of juniper and box on the vallum, and a solitary ancient beech surmounting the place of praetorium, presented nearly the same depths, heights, slopes and forms, which the Roman soldiers had originally given them. From this *castellum* Mr. Crotchet christened his villa. With his rustic neighbours he was of course immediately and necessarily a squire: Squire Crotchet of the castle; and he seemed to himself to settle down as naturally into an English country gentleman, as if his parentage had been as innocent of both Scotland and Jerusalem, as his education was of Rome and Athens.

The classical allusion brings Edward Gibbon back to mind, for as his great work charting the decline and fall of the Roman Empire was being published, the stage was being set for the demise of the English gentry's imperious rule over rural life. The manor house, though perhaps surviving as a habitable building, was soon to become a curiosity of a past way of life completely foreign to a democratic society, much as the Roman villa, once an expression of its owner's wealth and power, had become long before. But this is where we came in . . .

Some Manor Houses Open to the Public

Manor houses are listed here by county. Opening times and admission charges are not given, as they are liable to change, and intending visitors are advised to enquire before making long journeys or to consult the current *Guide to Historic Houses, Castles and Gardens*, published annually. Those houses where ownership is not given are still in private possession. A few manor houses mentioned in the book can be seen in part by virtue of now being hotels, restaurants etc, and several others are shown to architectural enthusiasts by private appointment.

Avon

Clevedon Court   (National Trust). Tel: 0172 872768. The house is between Bristol and Clevedon on B3130. There are car-parking facilities a short walking distance from the house, and tea and biscuits are available.

Horton Court   (National Trust). The house is one mile west of A46, three miles from Chipping Sodbury. Take Hawkesbury road from Horton village. Car-parking in front of the house, but no other facilities.

Buckinghamshire

Chenies Manor House. Tel: 0240 42888. The house is at the end of the lane past the church in the village of Chenies. Cars can be parked nearby, and tea and biscuits are available in the house.

Hughenden Manor (National Trust). Tel: 0494 32580. On A4128 between High Wycombe and Great Missenden. Car-park at side of house. Tea and biscuits served.

Waddesdon Manor (National Trust). Tel: 0296 65211. On A41 in the village of Waddesdon. Car-parking in front of house. Refreshments available.

Cheshire

Adlington Hall. Tel: 0625 829206. Off A523 five miles north of Macclesfield. Cars can be parked a short distance away. Tea and cakes are available.

Bramall Hall (Borough of Stockport). Tel: 0614 853708. The house is in Bramhall Park, one mile north of the village, off A5102. There is car-parking near the house, and refreshments are available in the adjoining café.

Gawsworth Hall. Tel: 0260 3456. In Gawsworth village, off A536 south-west of Macclesfield. Parking facilities in a field a few minutes' walking distance from the house, where there is also catering.

Little Moreton Hall (National Trust). Tel: 0260 22018. On A34 south of Congleton and unmissable. Cars can be parked in front of the house, where teas are served.

Cornwall

Antony House (National Trust). Tel: 0752 812191. The house is reached via the Torpoint car ferry from Plymouth and is on A374 two miles beyond landing-point. Parking a short distance from house, but no catering.

Cotehele (National Trust). Tel: 0579 50434. Off A390 west of Calstock. Car-parking near the house, where there is a good restaurant.

Ebbingford Manor. Tel: 0288 2808. The house is in Bude, signposted from the town centre. There are parking facilities in the grounds, and tea and biscuits are available.

Godolphin House. Tel: 0736 762409. Two miles off A394 between Godolphin Cross and Townshend. Car-parking near the house, where teas are served.

Old Post Office, Tintagel (National Trust). In the village. No parking or catering on the property, but both available in the village, close by.

Trerice (National Trust). Tel: 0637 35404. Secluded spot south-east of Newquay, reached by A3058 near Kestle Mill. Parking a short distance from house, where there is a restaurant.

Cumbria

Hutton in the Forest. Tel: 0853 4207. On B5305 six miles north-west of Penrith. Parking near the house, where refreshments are available.

Muncaster Castle. Tel: 0657 7614. The house is on A595 one mile south-east of Ravenglass. Cars are parked on the main road, some walking distance from the house, where there is a cafeteria.

Sizergh Castle (National Trust). Tel: 0448 60285. Beside A6, three miles south of Kendal. Car-parking near the house, but no catering.

Derbyshire

Haddon Hall. Tel: 0629 812855. Beside A6, two miles south-east of Bakewell. Car-park a few minutes walk from the house on main road. Catering in stables near the house.

Devon

Berry Pomeroy Castle (Ancient Monument). Tel: 0803 863397. The ruins are surrounded by woods two miles north-east of Totnes, reached by minor roads from A385. There are parking facilities and a café at the site.

Bradley Manor (National Trust). Tel: 0392 88345 (NT area office, Hele). Off A381 at western outskirts of Newton Abbot. Parking near the house; no catering.

Cadhay. Tel: 0404 812432. Off A30 one mile north of Ottery St Mary. Cars can be parked in an adjacent field. No catering.

Chambercombe Manor. Tel: 0271 62624. One mile south-east of Ilfracombe, off B3230. Car-parking on road near house, where lunches and teas are available.

Compton Castle (National Trust). Tel: 0804 72112. The 'castle' is four miles from Torquay, off A3022. Cars can be parked, but there is no catering.

Dartington Hall. Tel: 0803 862224. Off A384 two miles north-west of Totnes. Car-parking at the house, and restaurant at Cider Press Centre, nearby.

Dorset

Athelhampton Hall. Tel: 0305 84363. The house is on A35 east of Puddletown. Car-parking in grounds near the house. Teas available.

Purse Caundle Manor. Tel: 0963 250400. In the village of Purse Caundle, just off A30. Cars can be parked close to the house; no catering.

Wolveton House. Tel: 0305 3500. On A37 north-west of Dorchester. Parking among trees near entrance to the drive. No catering.

Essex

Layer Marney Towers. Tel: 0206 330202. Off B1022 at Smyth's Green, three miles north-east of Tiptree. Parking at gatehouse; no catering.

Gloucestershire

Chavenage House. Tel: 0666 52329. This isolated house stands on a minor road two miles north-west of Tetbury and is best reached by a left turn off A434 just beyond the town. Parking in front of the house; no catering.

Upper Slaughter Manor House. Tel: 0451 20927. The house is in the village, south-west of Stow-on-the-Wold. Limited parking in front of the house; no catering.

Hereford & Worcester

Eye Manor. Tel: 0568 85244. Off A49 four miles north of Leominster. There is parking space in front of the house, but no catering.

Harvington Hall. Tel: 0562 83267. Off A440 four miles south-east of Kidderminster. Parking on drive near the house, where refreshments are available.

Hellen's. The house is in Much Marcle village near the church. Cars can be parked there, but there is no catering.

Lower Brockhampton Manor (National Trust). Tel: 0885 22258. Off A44 two miles east of Bromyard, at the end of long, signposted drive. Parking near the house; no catering.

Hertfordshire

Salisbury Hall. Tel: 0727 23274. Beside A6, five miles south of St Albans. There are parking and refreshment facilities at the house.

Humberside

Burton Agnes Old Hall (Ancient Monument). Tel: 0262 89324. In the village, on A166 north-east of Great Driffield. Dwarfed by its Jacobean neighbour, in front of which cars can be parked and where refreshments are served.

Burton Constable. Tel: 0401 62400. On minor road north-east of Hull; reached by turn off B1238 at Sproatley. Parking a short walking distance from house, where there is a self-service cafeteria.

Isle of Wight
Arreton Manor. Tel: 0983 528134. The house is on A3056 two miles south-east of Newport. Car parking a short walking distance away. Lunches and teas available.

Kent
Hever Castle. Tel: 0732 862205. Off B2026, two miles east of Edenbridge. Car-parking facilities near house, where there is a large cafeteria.

Ightham Mote. Tel: 0732 62235. Just south of the hamlet of Ivy Hatch, off A227 four miles east of Sevenoaks. Limited parking a short distance from house; no catering.

Old Soar Manor (National Trust). This house is not easily found. It is best reached via Plaxtol, off A227 east of Sevenoaks, on minor road. Very little parking space and no catering.

Pattyndenne Manor. Tel: 0580 211361. The house is off B2037, south of Goudhurst. Parking on grass near house; no catering.

Penshurst Place. Tel: 0892 870307. In Penshurst village, seven miles south of Sevenoaks. Parking a short walking distance from house. Cafeteria adjacent.

Temple Manor (Ancient Monument). The house is near the centre of Strood, in Knight Road. Very limited parking space and no catering.

Lancashire
Browsholme Hall. Tel: 0254 86330. Four miles north-west of Clitheroe on the minor road to Whitewell. Parking in court-yard a few yards from house; no catering.

Chingle Hall. Tel: 0774 76216. On B5269 south-west of Goos-nargh. Limited parking on road; no catering.

Gawthorpe Hall (National Trust). Tel: 0282 66411. Off A671 on eastern outskirts of Padiham, at end of long drive. Parking in courtyard; teas available.

Hoghton Tower. Tel: 0254 852986. The house is on A675 five miles south-west of Burnley. Car-park in front of house; refreshments available.

Rufford Old Hall (National Trust). Tel: 0704 821254. On A59 six miles north of Ormskirk. Cars can be parked a few yards from the entrance, and teas are served in the house.

Samlesbury Hall (Samlesbury Hall Trust). Tel: 0254 812010. On A677 four miles east of Preston. Parking near the house, where there is a restaurant.

Leicestershire

Donington-le-Heath Manor (Leicestershire Museums). Tel: 0530 31259. In the village, one mile south-west of Coalville. Parking on road outside. Self-service catering.

Oakham Castle (Leicestershire Museums). Tel: 0572 3654. In the town centre, reached from market-place. Parking in the streets; no catering.

Quenby Hall. Tel: 0537 50224. The house lies east of Leicester on a minor road near Hungarton, off A47. Parking on grass in front of house. Self-service teas available.

Lincolnshire

Allington Manor House. Tel: 0400 5358. In the village of Allington north-west of Grantham. Car-parking on drive; no catering.

Doddington Hall. Tel: 0522 74227. In the village of Doddington, west of Lincoln. Parking in a field across the road; no catering.

Gainsborough Old Hall (Lincolnshire County Museums). Tel: 0427 2669. The house is in the centre of Gainsborough. Parking up to two hours near house; no regular catering.

Gunby Hall (National Trust). The house is on A158 2½ miles north-west of Burgh-le-Marsh. Parking nearby; no catering.

Tattershall Castle (National Trust). Tel: 0526 4253. On western outskirts of Tattershall village, on A153 between Sleaford and Horncastle. Parking a few yards from the house; no catering.

Woolsthorpe Manor (National Trust). In the village of Woolsthorpe, on A1 south of Grantham. Parking in adjacent farmyard; no catering.

Greater Manchester
Hall i' t' Wood (Bolton Metropolitan Borough). Tel: 0204 51159. On the northern fringe of Bolton, on turning off A58 bypass road. Limited parking near house; no catering.

Ordsall Hall (Salford Corporation). Tel: 0618 720251. The house is tricky to find on the south side of A57, two miles west of the centre of Manchester. Parking is possible in the street, but there is no catering.

Smithells Hall (Bolton Metropolitan Borough). Tel: 0204 21394. In a park whose entrance is from A6099, north of A58 bypass road. Parking near to house but no catering.

Merseyside
Speke Hall (National Trust). Tel: 0514 277231. Near Liverpool Airport, off A561 at Speke, south-east of city. Car-parking short distance from house; no catering.

Norfolk
Baconsthorpe Castle (Ancient Monument). The ruins are a mile along a farm track from the centre of the village, six miles south-west of Cromer. Parking but no catering.

Blickling Hall (National Trust). Tel: 0263 733471. On B1345 north-west of Aylsham on A140. Parking near the house, in which there is a restaurant.

Felbrigg Hall (National Trust). Tel: 0263 75444. Off A148 two miles south-west of Cromer. Parking in field a little walking distance away. Tea and cakes served.

Oxburgh Hall (National Trust). Tel: 0366 21258. Seven miles east of Downham Market on minor road leaving A134 at Stoke Ferry. Parking a little walking distance away. Teas available.

Northamptonshire
Aynhoe Park. Tel: 0869 810659. In the centre of Aynho village on A41. Limited parking in front of house; no catering.

Southwick Hall. Tel: 0832 6213. In village of Southwick on minor road three miles north of Oundle, between A43 and A605. Parking near house; no catering.

Sulgrave Manor. Tel: 0295 76205. In the village of Sulgrave eight miles north-east of Banbury off B4525. Cars can be parked beside the house; no catering.

Northumberland

Wallington Hall (National Trust). Tel: 0670 74283. In the village of
    Cambo, on B6342 west of Morpeth. Parking at the house,
    where there is a restaurant.

Oxfordshire

Broughton Castle. Tel: 0295 2624. The 'castle' is just off B4035, two
    miles south-west of Banbury. There is parking space near the
    church, and teas are sometimes available.
Greys Court (National Trust). Tel: 0491 7529. On minor road to
    Rotherfield Greys from Henley-on-Thames. Parking short
    walking distance from house; tea and biscuits sometimes
    available.
Mapledurham House. Tel: 0735 253350. Tucked away at the end of
    a long narrow lane off A4074, four miles north-west of Read-
    ing. Car-parking near the house, where teas are served.
Milton Manor. Tel: 0235 831287. In the village of Milton, south of
    Abingdon off B4016. Parking in a field near entrance; teas
    occasionally available.
Minster Lovell Hall (Ancient Monument). The ruins are reached
    via the churchyard in the village, five miles east of Burford.
    Car-parking is some distance away; no catering.
Stonor Park. Tel: 0491 63587. Off B480 between Henley-on-
    Thames and Watlington. Parking near house, where there is a
    tea-room.

Shropshire

Acton Burnell Castle (Ancient Monument). The ruins are in the
    village near the church, on minor road south-east of Shrews-
    bury between A49 and A458. Car parking in lane nearby; no
    catering.
Benthall Hall (National Trust). Tel: 0592 882254. The house lies off
    B4375 between Much Wenlock and Ironbridge. Parking in
    land nearby; no catering.
Shipton Hall. Tel: 0746 36225. In the village of Shipton on B4378
    six miles south-west of Much Wenlock. Parking in field a short
    distance from house; no catering.
Stokesay Castle. The 'castle' is just off A49, one mile south of
    Craven Arms. Car-park a short walking distance away; no
    catering.
Upton Hall. Tel: 0746 1307. Near village of Upton Cressett,

approached by a long, narrow road from A458 west of Bridg-north. Parking next to house; no catering.

Wilderhope Manor (National Trust). Tel: 0694 3363. On a minor road off B4371, seven miles south-west of Much Wenlock. Parking in yard nearby; no catering.

Somerset

Bardon Manor. Tel: 0984 4217. In Washford village, on A39 near Watchet. Parking in front of house, but no catering.

Barrington Court (National Trust). Tel: 0460 52242. On the out-skirts of Barrington village, three miles north-east of Ilminster. Parking in front of house; no catering.

Brympton d'Evercy. Tel: 0935 862528. Off A3088 two miles west of Yeovil. Parking in a field a few yards from front of house. Teas available.

East Lambrook Old Manor. Tel: 0460 40328. On B3165 north of South Petherton. Parking near the house, but no catering.

Gaulden Manor. Tel: 0984 7213. Tricky to find, the house is a mile east of Tolland church, off A358 Taunton–Williton road near Bishops Lydeard. Parking a short walking distance from house; there is a tea-room.

Halsway Manor (Halsway Manor Society). Tel: 0984 8274. Be-tween Bicknoller and Crowcombe on A361 six miles south-east of Watchet. Parking next to house; no catering.

Lytes Cary (National Trust). Tel: 0963 50586. The house is one mile off the A303 Ilchester bypass. Parking beside the house; no catering.

Midelney Manor. Tel: 0458 251229. Off A378 at Drayton near Curry Rivel, two miles south-west of Langport. Parking be-side the house; no catering.

Nunney Castle (Ancient Monument). The ruins are in the village, on A361 south-west of Frome. Cars can be parked in the street; no catering.

Suffolk

Kentwell Hall. Tel: 0787 25207. The house is in Long Melford village, on A134 north of Sudbury. Parking on grass a short walking distance from house, where refreshments are avail-able.

Melford Hall (National Trust). Also in Long Melford village, with parking facilities a short distance away. No catering.

Sussex, East

Great Dixter. Tel: 0797 43160. In the village of Northiam, off A28 twelve miles north of Hastings. Parking in field a little distance from the house; no catering.

Tyne & Wear

Washington Old Hall (National Trust). Tel: 0632 461454. In the village of Washington, six miles south of Newcastle. Cars can be parked in the street; no catering.

Warwickshire

Honington Hall. Tel: 0608 61434. On A34 one mile north of Shipston-on-Stour. Parking beside the house; no catering.

West Midlands.

Minworth Greaves Manor (Bournville Village Trust). Tel: 021 472 0199. Near the village green at Bournville, five miles south-west of Birmingham city centre. Parking in road; no catering.

Moseley Old Hall (National Trust). Tel: 0902 782808. The house is four miles north of Wolverhampton, three-quarters of a mile off A460. There are parking facilities, and teas are served.

Selly Manor House (Bournville Village Trust). Tel: 021 472 0199. Near village green at Bournville, as above.

Wightwick Manor (National Trust). Tel: 0902 761108. Off A454 three miles west of Wolverhampton. Free parking in front of house, but no catering.

Wiltshire

Avebury Manor. Tel: 0672 3203. In the village of Avebury, west of Marlborough. Parking only in the village, some distance from house; no catering.

Great Chalfield Manor (National Trust). In the village, which lies between Bradford-on-Avon and Melksham and is best reached by B3109. Parking near entrance; no catering.

Sheldon Manor. Tel: 0249 3120. On A420 a mile and a half to the west of Chippenham. Parking near the house. Tea and cakes available; other meals by arrangement.

Westwood Manor (National Trust). The house is in Westwood village, near Bradford-on-Avon. Cars can be parked inside the entrance gates, but there is no catering.

Yorkshire, North
Kiplin Hall. Tel: 0748 818290. On B6271 near Bolton-on-Swale, seven miles east of Richmond. Parking a short walking distance from the house, where tea and cakes are served.
Markenfield Hall. The house is along a farm road off A61 Ripon–Harrogate road. Park near farm buildings outside moat. No catering.
Nunnington Hall (National Trust). Tel: 0439 5283. On the outskirts of Nunnington village, off B1257 south-east of Helmsley. Parking near house, where tea and cakes are served.

Yorkshire, West
Oakwell Hall (Kirklees Metropolitan Council). Tel: 0924 474926. Off A652 Birstall-Dewsbury road, six miles from Leeds. Parking near house; no catering.

List of Sources

As well as the many topographical books I have consulted, and a few other works mentioned in the text, the following more specialized works have proved most helpful.

Michael Alexander (trans.). *Beowulf*, Penguin edition, 1973.
The Anglo-Saxon Chronicle. Everyman's Library edition, 1972.
Frank Barlow. *The Feudal Kingdom of England*, Longmans, 1955.
Bede. *Ecclesiastical History of the English Nation*, Everyman's Library edition, 1910.
S. T. Bindoff. *Tudor England*, Penguin, 1950
Geoffrey Chaucer. *The Canterbury Tales*, Oxford University Press, 1978 edition.
William Cobbett. *Rural Rides*, Everyman's Library edition, 1973.
H. C. Darby (ed.). *A New Historical Geography of England*, Cambridge University Press, 1973.
Sheppard Frere. *Britannia: A History of Roman Britain*, Routledge & Kegan Paul, 1967.
Mark Girouard. *Life in the English Country House*, Yale University, 1978.
Paul Hair (ed.). *Before the Bawdy Court*, Elek, 1972.
H. E. Hallam. *Rural England: 1066–1348*, Fontana, 1981.
Charles G. Harper. *Mansions of Old Romance*, Cecil Palmer, 1930.
W. G. Hoskins. *Provincial England*, Macmillan, 1963.
Richard Muir. *The Lost Villages of Britain*, Michael Joseph, 1982.
Nikolaus Pevsner and others. *The Buildings of England* (46 vols), Penguin, 1951–74.
A. L. Poole. *From Domesday Book to Magna Carta* (Oxford History of England), Oxford University Press, 1955.
Roy Porter. *English Society in the Eighteenth Century*, Penguin, 1982.
M. M. Postan. *The Medieval Economy and Society*, Weidenfeld & Nicolson, 1972.
D. M. Stenton. *English Society in the Early Middle Ages*, Penguin, 1951.
R. H. Tawney. *Religion and the Rise of Capitalism*, Penguin edition, 1938.
G. M. Trevelyan. *History of England*, Longmans, Green, 1926.
G. M. Trevelyan. *English Social History*, Longmans, Green, 1944.
John Warrington (ed.). *The Paston Letters*, Everyman's Library edition, 1975.
Dorothy Whitelock. *The Beginnings of English Society*, Penguin, 1952.
Margaret Wood. *The English Medieval House*, Ferndale edition, 1981.

Index